Manpower and Occupational Analysis: Concepts and Measurements

Manpower and Occupational Analysis: Concepts and Measurements

James G. Scoville
University of Illinois

Lexington Books
D.C. Heath and Company
Lexington, Massachusetts
Toronto   London

This research was conducted under a contract with the Office of Manpower Research, U.S. Department of Labor, under the authority of the Manpower Development and Training Act. Since contractors performing research under government sponsorship are encouraged to express their own judgment freely, the report does not necessarily represent the department's official opinion or policy. Moreover, the contractor is solely responsible for the accuracy of the data included in the report.

Reproduction in whole or in part permitted for any purpose of the United States government.

Contents

List of Tables

List of Figures

Introduction

Research for this volume was undertaken for a variety of reasons, with a wide range of goals in mind. In recent years, considerable improvements have been made in the occupational data available for public use—the new *Dictionary of Occupational Titles* and the expansion of census detail in 1970 can be cited. On the other hand, the publication of Shartle's *Occupational Information* in 1946 marks the last attempt to pull together all the various concepts and pieces of data, indicating their uses and significance. Such a survey is desirable in and of itself. Yet the present study tries to go beyond the stage of a user's handbook and to explore a number of related problems in the theory and measurement of work.

In the first place, what uses do social scientists, government agencies, business and labor groups, and other data consumers make of our occupational information? This facet of the subject area is interesting for its own sake, but carries with it a more fundamental objective. Most users of occupational data express their needs for new and improved concepts and figures more through their use of existing data than through responses to direct questioning. A survey of current applications is the best indicator of present and future requirements in the area. It is in this light that current data and proposed revisions are best understood.

The second chapter of the study covers several frequently used classification systems, with one eye upon their conceptual basis and the other upon practical shortcomings which characterize them. Insofar as this volume may be used as a reference work on the applicability of current data, it is felt crucial that both concepts and statistical difficulties be treated together. Comments on census, *Dictionary of Occupational Titles*, and *International Standard Classification of Occupations* information are followed by brief discussions of several proposals for amendment or improvement.

The arguments in Part 2 represent a marked change from most of the contents of this volume. The third chapter is addressed to development of an economic theory of the determination of the content of jobs and the relationships between various jobs within and between employing units.[a] I term this theory "economic" not because it ignores social and psychological factors—to which economists generally must turn for explanation of things that don't work in their models—but because it is based upon the cost and benefit conception of choice which is central to economic thinking. The model indicates the interests which employers and workers have in the concrete nature of jobs, develops the concept of human capital as it relates to training for work beyond the stage of Becker, and provides a theoretical framework for the models of job content and internal labor markets recently developed. The model-building exercise is fol-

[a]A briefer version of the model appeared in *Industrial Relations*, 9 no. 1 (October 1969), pages 36-53, as "A Theory of Jobs and Training."

lowed (in chapter 4) by several practical illustrations, which should emphasize the utility for analysis of a data scheme based upon this model.

In chapter 5, the desirable items of data to be collected are summarized in the light of the model, public policy information needs, and the goal of utility to researchers in general. The chapter is also addressed to questions of mechanics—how should improved data be obtained? Two competing possibilities are evaluated: employers (as suggested by the Gordon Committee in 1962) and workers (as is current practice). The conclusion that an improved household survey would offer the greatest hope is supported by doubts about the reliability or feasibility of detailed information from employers as much as by suggestions for the collection of better data from workers.

Development of the ideas and data reported in this volume followed two main avenues. In the first instance, most of the analysis of academic uses of occupational data was necessarily based upon the usual perusal of the literature. This approach was supplemented by a series of discussions with officials of companies, union, and government agencies, to yield insights on the usefulness of various kinds of data for research and operating purposes. The author wishes to express his gratitude to all those who gave of their time and knowledge toward the improvement of this study. These interviews and discussions were by no means intended to represent a random or extensive sample of the users of occupational data; hence, comments and reactions are strictly those of the persons and organizations involved. The general characteristics of those interviewed are very briefly outlined below.

Executives of companies	15
Officers of trade associations and industry groups	3
Research officers of labor unions	6
Officials of government agencies	17
Others: academic users, nonprofit organizations, consulting groups	6

It may seem curious to the reader that the theoretical section of this work (Part 2) comprises such a large fraction of its bulk. In part, this comes from the author's view that development of a conceptual basis for job-centered data is a critical aspect of the current debates about occupational and manpower information systems. Moreover, the theory is relevant to conceptualization and measurement of other aspects of the work/worker relationship—training requirements and worker mobility within the employing unit, determination of the content of specific jobs, and the allocation of training costs between workers and management. It is my feeling that Part 2 does, in fact, illuminate the discussions of other data schemes, provides an alternative—and more generally applicable and transferable—conceptual framework, and lends support to the specific new data forms requested in Part 3.

I am indebted to John Dunlop for his continuing interest in accurate description of the jobs performed by the labor force, and for stimulating discussions of the theory of job breadth. Innumerable colleagues at Harvard and in the Boston area commented on various parts of earlier drafts. Finally, I am deeply grateful to Tony, the proprietor of the Varsity Sub Shop in Cambridge, for sustenance in support of this research.

James G. Scoville
Champaign, Illinois
December 1971

Part 1: Occupational Data and Their Uses

1

A Survey of the Uses of Occupational Data

The various academic disciplines impose diverse burdens upon our manpower and occupational data, as do analysts in business, government, and education who are concerned with the planning and development of manpower, of social programs, of educational facilities. The survey of this chapter explores some of the ends to which these data are applied, beginning with social scientists. In general, it should be read as much for guidelines of need and desired improvements as for a catalog of current applications. "More detail at more frequent intervals" is a general desire, but one which doesn't get us very far down the road towards better utilization of scarce statistical resources.

As a word of caution: many of the requests and needs expressed by analysts from other disciplines have been gauged and evaluated through the perceptions of an economist. It is not unlikely that sociologists and political scientists would view the problems somewhat differently, or would at least express them in different language.

Economists

The uses to which economists have put our occupational information are widely varied, so naturally the needs which are felt for expansion and improvement in that data base are correspondingly diverse. Let us briefly enumerate some of the major areas of concern where these statistics are of importance.

With regard to education and training, such data have found themselves at the center of empirical research. Thus, the school of thought associated with analysis of "human capital" has relied extensively upon time streams of occupational earnings to estimate the returns to investment in human beings.[1] In attempts to measure the costs and returns of apprenticeship programs in the construction trades, Mincer was compelled, by using existing data, to make comparisons which are not entirely appropriate.[2]

On a somewhat different track, economists and others have attempted to evaluate the educational and training requirements associated with occupations. The census educational attainment data are clearly of little use in exercises of this sort, although such figures may be relevant to the flexibility of the labor force and other broader characteristics of social life. The only requirements estimates covering all jobs are found in the third edition of the *Dictionary of Occupational Titles* (henceforth referred to as *DOT*), evolving from estimates pub-

3

lished for a sample of jobs in 1956.[3] Despite the strictures of those in the BES who developed these numbers, the temptation to translate them into required years of schooling eventually proved too great. First Eckaus on an industrial basis,[4] then Scoville on an occupational basis,[5] made the translation. It should be noted that Eckaus' task was easier and presumably less prone to error—the 1956 education and training numbers were associated with an industrial code. Errors and misclassifications entered the present author's work due to the lack of a convertibility list between *DOT* codes and census occupations. A variety of other criticisms against such translations have been advanced by Sidney Fine.[6]

Nevertheless, the point is clear: for assessment of the impact of future employment patterns on the educational and training systems of the country, data of this sort are needed. One may be skeptical of the value and accuracy of the *DOT* estimates;[7] one may be grateful that *DOT* census conversion tables are now being developed; but those are separable problems. The fundamental need is for requirements estimates; this seems likely to be met in the near future, although conceptual difficulties inherent in the nature of estimating requirements will remain.

An analogous need in construction of certain economic models centers upon input coefficients for the various types of labor which would appear in a more complete input-output model.[8] Evidently, an occupation-by-industry matrix which appears only for each census is of limited sensitivity for problems of this sort. Moreover, much clearer specification of the technology and associated job mixes is necessary for analysis of the technical and economic factors leading to changes in input coefficients. It is particularly in analysis of these problems that the "economic principles of occupational classification" should hold true—that elasticities of substitution and cross-elasticities of labor supply be higher within the groups than between them.[9]

Occupational information which bears some relationship to relative levels of "skill"—or more broadly, to levels of job content—is required to assess wage and earnings differentials and the forces which influence them. The major census groups (and most of the detailed ones as well) are hardly satisfactory, but they represent the only format in which overall employment estimates are available. Similarly, analyses of the growth in real wages, or the creation of production functions with disaggregated labor inputs, require improved information of this sort.

Much the same can be said for analysis of labor mobility. The current groupings do not reflect homogeneous kinds of labor or embrace similar enough jobs to make defensible the measures which were developed during the "structuralist" debate of the early 1960s. Thus, to cite one example, a test of labor market efficiency which uses income and unemployment data for major census groups can hardly be considered conclusive.[10] The need for meaningful job categories to assess worker mobility patterns, not surprisingly, runs parallel to the desire for some information on the substitutability or complementarity of various jobs and skill constellations.

To assess the pure impact of race on income, it is necessary to standardize for work performed, among many other factors. Census groups have been used for this purpose, which require some heroic assumptions about their social and economic homogeneity.[11]

Considerable interest is attached to the growth and determinants of union membership. Until recently, we had only infrequent information on the characteristics of union members, and that in no great detail.[12] Moreover, much greater quantities of information on the job, its content, technology, and environment, would be required to fully evaluate the factors and conditions which influence individuals' decisions union membership.

Integration of the labor force qua body of consumers into economic model-building is relatively rare. One example is found in the work of Clopper Almon, where an attempt is made on the demand side (via the generation of labor incomes) to justify the industry outputs flowing from his production model.[13] More generally, consumption-income relationships will be affected by the dispersion and distributions of incomes among various segments of the labor force.

Sociologists

This particular sector of the social sciences is probably second to none in its utilization of various kinds of occupational information. Often these data are based upon broad, familiar, commonsense occupations which seem appropriate to the study at hand. On the other hand, the frequency of use of census classifications and data is extremely high. The following areas of interest in sociological research for which occupational information is important, as well as the studies cited, are largely taken from a brief survey of the prominent journals in several recent years. By any index, utilization of census data is extensive: one can only speculate on reasons for the virtual absence of demands for better data exhibited by practitioners in this field.

A principal area of concern, reflected by Jerome Gordon's proposal summarized in chapter 2, centers upon the *status* or *prestige* characteristics of various occupations or social groups. A number of efforts to evaluate social economic status and to identify its determinants are summarized in Blau and Duncan's recent volume, *The American Occupational Structure.*[14] At the same time, they present a regression of survey results on status against corresponding census education and income data, which shows status as dependent upon these variables. In this regard, one might have wishes that the detailed census titles were themselves more homogeneous, so that the congruence of one "common knowledge" occupation in their opinion survey with the census "bundle of occupations" would be more exact.

In a similar kind of study, Hollingshead and Redlich both supplemented and altered the occupational classification to produce an "Index of Social Position." For them, occupation—even when redefined as "social-economic group" by

Edwards—was an insufficient indicator of social class. Not only did measures of residential location and educational attainment have to be added for the final index, but some measure of degree of authority associated with an occupation had to be developed. To this end, the Edwards groups were reshuffled according to the size of enterprise or number of subordinate workers directed.[15]

Concerns with prestige have not remained confined to the domestic American scene. In 1956, Inkeles and Rossi found close correspondence among the prestige rankings of various industrialized nations.[16] In this case, for the limited number of well-known occupations which they used, one can expect a reasonable degree of consistency across national boundaries in the nature of the work performed associated with each title.

One of the most recent developments in this area should emphasize the need for a set of comparable classifications between societies, but suggests to this writer that the task may be extraordinarily difficult. When dealing with societies at different ends of the development spectrum, individuals in the same "generic" occupations and/or prestige groups simply may not do exactly comparable work. Thus, Armer recently found strong similarities between prestige rankings in the United States and in Hausaland (Northern Nigeria).[17] The author admits that there are no perfect correspondences between the two lists of occupations,[18] although to be fair, it should be conceded that there are strong resemblances between many of the paired occupations. These resemblances may, however, be more characteristic of prestige than of work performed. Note the following selected comparisons from Armer's list: could any list of comparable titles be developed which adequately reflected the differences in life styles which surround the performance of these general functions? The development of comparable job descriptions may thus be a somewhat different task than that of creating measures of métier.

Hausaland	U.S.
Mallams	Clergyman
Market Traders	Retail Salesmen
Leather Workers	Craftsmen—Shoemakers or Laborers in leather products
Praise-singers and Drummers	Laborers—personal services

Closely related to measurement of the status and prestige of various occupations is the evaluation of the "distance"—social and cultural—between them. The distance between occupations should affect a variety of other variables—occupational change and mobility, patterns of association and friendship, and an individual's behavior as a result of change from one status level to another, to name but a few. Most of these studies rely on published data or classifications.

Two general approaches seem to have been employed to measure distance. In the first case, scales can be set up based upon survey perceptions of status differences as related to measurable economic-social and economic variables.[19] Once the rankings have been developed, analysis can proceed on a wide front. The second approach involves the inference of distances from the ease or difficulty of making the transition from one occupational group to another. In such cases the need for a "status dimensionality" among occupations is avoided.[20] For either approach to be usefully applied to census data, there must be some assurance that the published groupings are reasonably homogeneous in terms of status and that, if they are not, no major shifts in the importance of subgroups takes place over time.

In order that the need for a sound set of data underlying these analyses be most clearly seen, a brief catalog of the recent applications of distance measures may be of value. Studies have focused upon possible effects on mental health of certain status changes,[21] urban residential and friendship patterns,[22] and participation in community organizations by persons of differing occupational status.[23] Other studies have centered upon defense of economic status by white male workers through economically rational discrimination against women and Negroes,[24] and the factors influencing the geographical mobility of various classes of workers.[25] The foregoing should indicate the richness of the research being developed in this area; let us recall that for the most part the accuracy of the results depends directly on whether the underlying census data mean what the authors assume.

Another area of concern in sociological journals has been with the measurement of community power structures and concentrations. In order to indicate the use of census occupational data in this regard—and to suggest that their serious deficiencies were not sufficiently recognized—allow me to summarize one brief dispute.

Several years ago, Hawley argued that centralization of power in a community would directly affect that community's ease of adoption and progress on plans for urban renewal.[26] His reasoning and method need not detain us—what is important is the measure which he chose for power concentration. Hawley claimed that the smaller the fraction of census "managers, officials, and proprietors," in the city's labor force, the more was power concentrated in a few hands. I suggest that there are a great number of things wrong with this measure: a number of classes of people with considerable power and influence (lawyers, ministers) are excluded, while persons largely irrelevant to power concentrations (railroad conductors, ship's officers) are included. A more fundamental objection might argue that, in some cases, the number of these people is unrelated to the concentration of power. Thus, the proportion of union officers (included in the census managerial group) is presumably more tied to kinds of unions prominent in an area, as well as to whatever power these unions may be able to exert.[27]

Some of these deficiencies in the data base were not lost upon critics of Hawley's work. Straits cited many of the peculiar exclusions and inclusions noted above, and concluded (although for different reasons) that the fraction of the labor force classed as "managers, etc., should be the *least* accurate index of the number of policy makers in the power structure at the apex. . . ."[28] In this entire literature survey this is one of the few cases that I have found of criticisms based upon use of inappropriate social or occupational classifications. Perhaps most significant is the fact that Hawley's reply to Straits does not take this issue to be a serious one.[29]

It may perhaps seem curious to fellow economists that a number of recent articles in sociological journals have "poached" upon a venerable part of our preserve—the division of labor. Nonetheless, sociological concern with the effects of the organization of productive activities upon social organization goes at least as far back as Weber.[30] One facet of this is reflected in a recent study of the impact of technology on the structure and organization of the surrounding productive enterprise.[31]

Two recent studies have taken a closer look at definition and effects of the division of labor per se, and have in both cases relied upon census data for estimates. In the first study, Galle found that the size of cities and their industrial specialization affected their occupational composition.[32] The author admits quite freely that his data groups are heterogeneous,[33] but we might well ask how sensitive a measure of division of labor (in the sense of Adam Smith or F.W. Taylor) results from the categories employed. Galle's groups are five in number: professional, technical, etc.; managers, etc.; clerical; sales; and all blue collar. It would seem that by far the greatest amount of true division of labor must take place *within* these groups, rather than be reflected *among* them.

A more recent study puts the problem in a different light and, more important, serves to emphasize the critical distinction between the concepts of "job" and "occupation."[34] To which of these phenomena—job or occupation—does the process of division of labor apply? Clearly, the answer must be that division of labor affects the content and breadth of concrete jobs in production situations, and does not necessarily affect the contents of that species of related jobs which we know as an "occupation." Most certainly, the concept does not apply to occupations as currently measured by the Census.

Specifically, consider the measure of division of labor utilized by Gibbs and Browning:

$$D_i = 1 - \frac{\Sigma(x^2)}{(\Sigma x)^2},$$

where x is employment in each *occupational* group. The authors state, "where everyone in a particular industry has the same occupation, the degree of division of labor within that industry is at a minimum; and where persons are evenly distributed throughout the occupations within an industry, the division of labor within that industry is at a maximum."[35] I would argue that the contents of census occupations are so disparate as to make this an insensitive index at best. Moreover, in view of the fact that division of labor is comprehensible *only* in terms of specific *jobs*, the statement is incorrectly applied to *occupations*. I can conceive of industries in which the division of labor—in the economic and technical sense—has proceeded very far, with almost all workers performing very narrow, repetitive tasks, which would rank perversely by this index. After all, the entire work force would fall into one occupational group— low skilled highly subdivided operations—no matter how detailed the latter classification. We would have no idea from the Gibbs-Browning index of the lengths to which task subdivision had gone.

Since division of labor seems to play a role in diverse areas of sociological inquiry, the interests of sociologists in better data would seem to conform with those of other social scientists. An appropriate measure of the division of labor, as with measures of job content or training requirements, can only come with a clearer focus upon job information as the basic unit of data. Occupations, social groups, and classes, and other categories can then be built up according to their own internal principles, rather than forcing a given set of data to perform tasks to which those data are ill-suited.

Political Scientists

Here, as elsewhere, the classifications of scholarly workers and work fields are now necessarily congruent. Persons who are not, strictly speaking, political scientists, do address themselves to problems of political behavior. Hence the lowly economist will perhaps be forgiven if he places primary emphasis upon work performed, and relies less upon job titles and questions of academic jurisdiction.

Some part of the relevance of occupations to political analysis can be given in the words of Lipset:

Occupationally determined activities affect not only the individual's participation in the organized communications network of society, and hence his consciousness of political issues, but also his ability to engage in political activity.[36]

Thus, an individual may be precluded by his occupation from political action due to lack of leisure time, "or, even more important, *psychic* leisure time free of anxieties that can be devoted to non-personal problems."[37] Lipset summarizes a variety of foreign studies which bear upon the relationship between voting participation and occupational or social class.[38]

This type of analysis can be pushed somewhat further, and we mention some additional material from Lipset to illustrate the point. For example, what needs of mankind are frustrated by the characteristics of certain jobs, to produce *particular patterns* of voting or other political activity? The suggestion is made that those occupations characterized by (*a*) insecurity of income streams from seasonal or cyclical causes; (*b*) work which is monotonous or otherwise unsatisfactory or frustrating; and (c) low in status; should be characterized by substantial left-wing sentiment and support.[39]

Along the same lines, relatively crude occupational classifications were used by Lipsitz in his study of the attitudes of workers in an automobile plant, where "assembly line workers" were found to be more fatalistic, punitive, and politically radical than other groups of workers in the same plant.[40] The relatively common use of the proportion of the labor force in professional and managerial occupations as an index of social status was continued by Reiselbach in his study of the relationship between a congressman's votes on foreign aid and the status of his constituents.[41] Information on the attendant characteristics of human work—physical and mental fatigue, isolation, and hazards of the workplace, the nature of the plant and its management, hours and scheduling of work, variability of income—appear as relevant variables in these and similar models of political behavior, much as they appear in the model of job content developed in chapter 3. In spite of the fact that quite often these characteristics can be readily adduced (at least in general terms)—for example, the coal miners, fishermen, lumbermen, and Australian sheepshearers mentioned by Lipset—they have hardly reached a satisfactory stage of quantification. Thus, one would be hard put to create a time-series index of leftism-producing variables. The problem remains that some parts of the desired data are found in one place, some elsewhere, some not at all. Even for those pieces of information readily available, the categories and classifications are seldom easily comparable.

The above survey indicates that occupations form a significant, if small, part of theories and measures of political power and behavior. The major census groups are often used as indicators of the social or employment status of individuals or groups, and quite frequently (as with use of the whole "professional" or "managerial" categories) this use reflects an ignorance of the contents of these groups. That ancillary information on the conditions surrounding jobs and workers seems essential is also apparent. Political scientists seem to have been less concerned—or less vocal—about their needs for improved data, but the trend toward empirical analysis and behavior work in this field should reverse the situation.

Lessons from the Ivory Tower

The preceding short surveys of several social sciences leave the reader with certain conclusions about academic needs for data. Most of them pertain to the finding that current occupational data are not equally suitable for all purposes. Thus, we find outright misuse of the figures as proxies for things which they do not measure. Important as this finding may be to forewarn future users, the literature surveys provide us with a more valuable suggestion. For most scholarly analysis, the emphasis in any revision of the data should be placed upon increased detail and improved systems of classifications, and not upon radically increased frequency. None of the studies, for example, appears to require detailed data on a monthly basis. When academic researchers express desires for greater frequency, they have their eyes upon the decennial census as a point of departure, not upon the CPS as a goal.

Let us now turn to data uses and needs in the "real world."

Vocational Education

The primary informational need expressed by those responsible for planning vocational education concerns the identification of areas of training which have relatively broad applicability. There is widespread recognition that training for specific jobs does not produce workers with sufficient flexibility to adapt to economic and technological change. Unfortunately, there does not appear to be available a generally accepted set of skill groupings which would facilitate planning curricula and programs.

In this context one can cite the experience of a group making concrete plans for the construction of a new vocational high school in a large Eastern city. This group was confronted very clearly by the need to escape from the narrow specialization which had characterized its past course program, but was unsure of the path to be followed toward broader training. They observed that current information, in particular the *Occupational Outlook Handbook* series, was of very little use, as it retained the emphasis on specificity.

Another attempt to utilize commonly available information to identify occupational training families has been summarized by Frantz. In his study, an attempt was made to define "clusters" of occupations for which specific vocational training curricula could be developed. An extended quotation reflects the need for balance between specificity and generality in training, and summarizes an effort to employ the *DOT* in this connection.

The third edition of the *Dictionary of Occupational Titles (D.O.T.)* was carefully scanned for possible use of existing occupational groupings developed from observation and analysis of jobs over the last twenty-five years. It seemed at first that the two-digit divisions, established on the basis of work fields, materials and products, would represent the most feasible occupational families. However, a further examination of both the divisions and the three-digit classifications within the divisions revealed some occupational groupings that were too narrowly defined to encompass the wide range of jobs necessary in a cluster concept program (for example, Division 81: Welders, Flame Cutters, and Related Occupations). On the other hand, some occupations that are related on the basis of work fields were found in separate divisions (for example, Division 65: Printing Occupations; and Division 97: Occupations in Graphic Arts). For these reasons, the *D.O.T.* divisions, with the possible exception of construction, were rejected as unsuitable for our purposes.[42]

The Massachusetts Advisory Council on Education, as part of an effort to reform vocational training in that state, developed the following *ad hoc* list of major occupational clusters:

> Building and construction
> Transportation and power
> Business and office
> Distribution occupations
> Health occupations
> Industrial and fabrication
> Foods and kindred
> Agricultural occupations
> Communications, information storage and retrieval[43]

It should be noted that these clusters are quite broad, frequently embracing a large number of distinct trades, yet possessing certain training commonalities.

In the absence of general information on training clusters, other attempts have been made to evaluate the training core of various areas and specialties.[44] Such studies serve to emphasize the need for some discussion of a new occupational classification which would reflect the relationships between jobs in terms of training commonalities, promotion and mobility patterns, and the balance between general and vocational education.

These needs have been underscored by the 1968 amendments to the Vocational Education Act which require the states to create five-year detailed plans with a firm data base. One secondary vocational school administrator, faced with the deadline for such a plan, confessed that the numbers just were not there. The BLS occupation/industry matrix, coupled with forecasts of industrial employment, was of some value in predicting total employment levels by occupation. Unfortunately, there were no figures on expected replacement needs from attrition, which (in that particular state) were likely to exceed net increments for most skilled jobs.

Government Agencies

For the most part, agencies at the several levels of government tend to view their needs for new or improved data in the light of their own operating or research needs. Only occasionally are broader, more fundamental interests expressed.

Several years ago, Dr. Margaret Martin of the Bureau of the Budget circularized a number of agencies on changes and expansions of available occupational statistics. Typical of the replies were the following:

1. More data on technicians (from a branch of the Office of Emergency Planning)

2. More detail on office machine operators (from a number of agencies)
3. Information on foreign military personnel and government officials (from the Immigration and Naturalization Service)
4. More data on the range and concentration of income by occupations (from OEO)

A number of the replies which are closely related to agency research needs would nevertheless add to our knowledge of the associated characteristics of jobs and occupations. Although some responses evidenced ignorance of currently available data, some of the more ingenious and challenging requests may be briefly summarized:

1. More information on physical demands and psychological stress (from a branch of the National Institutes of Health)
2. Data on job content, qualifications requirements, and the components of compensation (from the Civil Service Commission)
3. Data on the difficulty of jobs and ease of substitution of workers between them (from the Federal Reserve)
4. Insistence that our data be more closely comparable with internationally applicable systems (such as ISCO)–(from a branch of the Executive Office of the President concerned with foreign economic affairs)

Some federal agencies expressed wishes for things that would make their life easier: for example, the Joint Economic Committee staff placed primary emphasis upon the retention of historical comparability in any revision. Similar requests or criteria based on particular research or operational needs typified some of the author's interviews for the present study. Thus, state and area planning organizations desire forecasts of the kinds and numbers of workers which the school systems must train.

Not all data requirements are so well verbalized. One of the more recent needs in this area to be revealed by the federal government is in the area of skill levels, training times, and training costs. This range of problems has arisen with the growth of training programs aimed at the disadvantaged coupled with programs to encourage employers to perform the required training. The lack of appropriate data has recently led the government to what must be the most peculiar use of DOT information on the record.

In a pamphlet published by JOBS–National Alliance of Businessmen,[4][5] the following procedure is outlined for reimbursement of employers' training costs. The contractor is instructed to sum the last three digits of the DOT code, that is, the figures pertaining to levels of function with regard to "Data," "People," and "Things." This sum is then an (inverse) measure of "Skill Level"; the permissible range for MA-4 training contracts is between skill levels 10 and 20. For jobs at level 10 (e.g. hopgrower, alligator farmer, toolmaker), 1760 hours of training will be reimbursed at half the hourly rate; for jobs at level 20 (brokerage clerks, touchup painter, hat blocker), the figure is 680 hours. Intermediate hours are applied to skill levels between the two end points.

The reader is referred to the third section of chapter 2 for a fuller discussion of the existing "Data," "People," and "Things" scales. With more specific reference to the matter of training times and reimbursements, let us note the following questions:

1. Are the individual scales linear?
2. Are the three scales' factors equally costly in terms of training?
3. Are all aspects of jobs which affect training *times* included?
4. Are all aspects of jobs which affect training *costs* (e.g. wastage of materials, foregone product, supervision) included?

For this measure to be a valid approximation to training costs, all of the foregoing questions must be answered "more or less, yes." I suspect that the answer in each case should be "no." In the interests of the proper allocation of training funds, it would appear that the Manpower Administration has a considerable need for actual estimates of the components of training costs associated with particular jobs or occupations.[46]

It is not our purpose to abuse the Manpower Administration or Labor Department by bringing forward this example of data misuse. Other examples certainly could be found elsewhere, although probably not in an agency which is itself so concerned with development of appropriate measures of manpower utilization and need. Rather, the point is to underscore the difference between the real data needs expressed by operating programs, and the relatively bland, inoffensive needs for data reported to outside inquirers.

Uses of Occupational Data in Business Enterprises

Firms utilize external occupational information in a variety of ways, although their most valued data come from internal sources or interfirm exchanges of employment and wage rate figures. On balance, current occupational data are of limited utility to businessmen.

At the outset, we note that one part of the government's array of occupational materials is in general disuse among employers. Most of the people interviewed had more than a passing familiarity with the *Dictionary of Occupational Titles*, but were not putting it to any use. Reasons for this are spelled out in more detail in chapter 5, but the prime complaint was the *DOT*'s lack of industry—or firm—specificity. It simply does not contain sufficient detail to embrace the exact jobs appearing in the various establishments. Dictionaries for various industries or trade groups were suggested by several companies, perhaps arranged not in the present alphabetical manner, but by family groupings around industry subdivisions and specific technological components of the production process.

With regard to other occupational data, the most important use—judging by frequency of mention, as well as complaints about numbers currently available—centers upon questions of plant location. An airline considering location of a new maintenance facility observed that figures on labor availability were of crucial importance. In planning the new installation, they utilized data on labor force composition and unemployment rates, supplemented by an analysis of local USES[a] job and applicant files. The firm stated that insufficient corollary information was available on the comparative characteristics of local labor forces—absenteeism, turnover, training backgrounds—which would strongly affect their choice of location.

Several other companies planning new facilities were more typical: they complained that current data were irrelevant. Only the general labor market trends reported in the Manpower Report were of any use, according to one respondent. The reason for this reaction, in contrast to that of the airline, is not hard to find. The manpower needs of these companies were much more varied, ranging from common laborers to managers; the airline, by and large, was concerned with only one range of skills—mechanics. These more typical companies felt the need for greater occupational detail, more frequent data, and greatly improved workforce characteristics estimates. In this respect, they echoed the conclusions of an NPA Technical Workshop that detailed occupational data by sex, turnover, and unemployment would be an essential part of the regional information needed for accurate decisions on plant location.[47]

Sundry other applications of employment and labor force data were reported by the companies interviewed. Unemployment rates (and projections of them) were valuable parts of marketing plans and surveys. Occupational data are of value to life insurance companies for both actuarial and marketing purposes. One manufacturing company used the BLS Area Wage Surveys to set wage scales in its small, nonunion establishments. However, in general, labor force, employment, and related data are distinctly of secondary concern to businesses: most companies interviewed made no use of them at all other than as another indication of the overall economic situation. This conclusion corresponds well with the results of an NPA survey on the utilization of projections and estimates by firms summarized in Table 1-1.[48] About half of those using this kind of information reported using it "little."

Table 1-1

Comparative Utilization of Various Types of Data

Type of Information	% Firms Using Data	Degree of Use		
		Great	Moderate	Little
Population & Demographic Characteristics	80	33	33	17
Labor Force Data	71	11	26	34
GNP & Components	83	32	38	13
Personal Income	75	22	32	20
FRB Index	72	20	27	26

[a]United States Employment Service, now USTES—United States Training and Employment Service.

Uses and Needs—Overview

The conclusion which results from a survey of "real world" data users is substantially the same as that which came from the social science applications reviewed. In any data revisions, our goals should focus primarily on increases in degree of detail regarding specific kinds of jobs, their technological and social contexts, and their associated educational, training, and income characteristics. Less emphasis should be placed upon increases in frequency: interest in increased frequency falls off rapidly for intervals less than one year. Although frequencies greater than that may be desirable for other reasons, the verdict of those interviewed places the stress on detail, particularly the measurement of new dimensions of jobs.

2

Current Schemes and Proposed Reforms

The task of this chapter is to explore the conceptual bases of several types of currently available data (census, *DOT*, ISCO) as well as the principles behind several proposed revisions of the classificatory structure. In passing, several observations are made about the practical applicability and accuracy of the information now in use. In as much as practical drawbacks flow in general from difficulties in the conceptual frameworks, such discussion is by no means irrelevant. Moreover, a heightened awareness of such problems may have two beneficial results: to reduce the incidence of data misuse, and to foster concern for better data among social scientists.

Dictionary of Occupational Titles (DOT)

The *Dictionary of Occupational Titles*, developed by the Bureau of Employment Security, U.S. Department of Labor, is currently in its third edition. It represents an approach to the area of occupational information different from most of the systems discussed below. Although the parallel is not exact, a useful analogy can be drawn between census information pertaining to workers and the *DOT*, which is a partial census of jobs. In this sense, it is an index of the number of broad bundles of specific jobs (which bundles are termed occupations) existing in significant quantity throughout the U.S. economy. The *Dictionary* also includes a great deal of additional information about job characteristics, broad families of occupations and work fields. We shall first turn our attention to the basic data and their organization.

Historical Development of the DOT. The present Federal-State system of employment services was established in 1933 by the Wagner-Peyser Act. The various states established employment services, funded largely by federal money, which handle unemployment compensation, as well as requests and applications from employers and workers. The *DOT* was a natural by-product of the placement functions of agencies affiliated with the United States Employment Service.

In the mid-1930s, the Bureau of Employment Security began the direct study of jobs existing in American industry. Since that time the number of separate jobs analyzed has surpassed one-hundred thousand. By 1937, a sufficient number of studies had been carried out to permit the development of an overall, economy-wide listing. The first edition of the *Dictionary* appeared in 1939; during World War II a variety of supplementary documents were published. Most notable was a separate volume focusing on entry jobs which reflected the wartime production requirements necessitating the integration of new kinds of workers into the industrial labor force. In 1949, a second edition of the *DOT* was issued.

In rough terms, the same occupational classification system was employed in the first two editions of the *Dictionary*. The job groupings were intended to represent an "occupational-industrial breakdown" of the jobs in our economy, in which work performed was classified by seven basic groups: professional and managerial; clerical and sales; service; agricultural, skilled occupations; semi-skilled occupations; and unskilled occupations. Although the stated purpose of occupational-industrial groupings differs from the census' goal of social-economic groups, the names and contents of the principal groups were remarkably similar.

The Third Edition of the DOT. Sixteen years elapsed between the compilation of the 1949 *Dictionary* and its successor. Although one of the common complaints about the *DOT* is the infrequency of its publication, the time between the two editions allowed considerable experimentation and revamping of *Dictionary* concepts.

The raw material of the *Dictionary* consists of 21,741 separately defined occupations, which are presented in volume 1 of the 1965 edition. These are the basic building blocks of the occupational classification to which the traits, aptitudes, and training characteristics refer. Each of these defined occupational titles actually represents a broad bundle of specific jobs which the BES personnel have analyzed. It is recognized that the same general type of job will vary from plant to plant, depending on a wide range of factors. Thus, the definitions in the *Dictionary's* first volume usually end with a series of "may" statements about work elements which fall with varying frequencies into the general occupation. The variability of these probabilistic elements of job content, and the factors (such as crew size or plant age) upon which they may depend, are not spelled out.

Occupational Classification Systems of the DOT

The basic defined atoms of the *Dictionary* are structured in two different classifications—an occupational classification and a worker traits arrangement. The latter reflects groupings of jobs which require similar abilities, aptitudes, and work preferences on the part of persons in these jobs. Its primary purpose is to facilitate the placement function of matching job demands and worker attributes.

The occupational classification of the third edition of the *DOT* is somewhat different from its predecessors'. The occupational groups are based on "a combination of work field, purpose, material, product, subject matter, service, generic term, and/or industry."[1] The major groups to which occupations are assigned are listed in Table 2-1 below, along with a summary of the particular factors listed above which seem to predominate in the categorization by two- and three-digit occupational groups.

A number of observations should be made about this occupational classification. The most significant changes from 1949 involve the new blue-collar groups 5-8, wherein the former explicit skill groupings have been discarded in favor of groups based upon kinds of work performed. Moreover, the structure shown above embodies an approach to occupational classification which recognizes that the significant characteristics of various jobs differ. For professional workers of many kinds, the subject matter dealt with is an appropriate division point, just as the nature of a sales job depends on what (doughnuts or insurance) and how (auctioneers vs. sales ladies in department stores) one is selling. The recognition that the core of identifying characteristics which tie together specific jobs into occupations varies widely across the job structure is an important step forward.

Table 2-1

Important Factors in the Occupational Classification of the DOT

Major Group	2 Digit Level	3 Digit Level
0. Professional	Subject matter	More detailed subject matter
1. Technical & Managerial Occupations	Function (managing)	Industry
2. Clerical & Sales Occupations	Types of activity Service vs. product; Technique of selling	More specific activity or equipment Commodities or services sold; detailed method of selling
3. Service Occupations	Type of service	Specific occupational or industrial type of service
4. Farming, Fishery, Forestry, & related Occupations	Products	Products and activities
5. Processing Occupations	Work field,	More specific work field, material, product, or work group
6. Machine Trades Occupations	Material	
7. Bench-work Occupations	or	
8. Structural Work Occupations	Product	
9. Miscellaneous Occupations	Industry (primarily)	Functions within industry

Source: Material culled from the 1965 *Dictionary of Occupational Titles*, vol. 1, pp. xvii-xviii and vol. 2, pp. 1-24.

One is less certain, though, that the principles enunciated have been success-fully applied to all jobs in the *Dictionary*. Concern immediately centers upon group 9: "Miscellaneous Occupations." Many of the titles there are involved in transport and utilities, some are in mining and amusements, and most strangely, logging, which might more naturally have gone with forestry in group 4.[a] The need to compress the whole occupational structure into ten major groups—which is virtually inescapable with a decimal coding system—may explain some of these anomalies.

This particular constraint is not found in the *Dictionary's* second occupation-al distribution, the "Worker Traits Arrangement." In this system, the basic de-fined occupations "are grouped according to some combination of required gen-eral educational developments, specific vocational preparation, aptitudes, inter-ests, temperaments, and physical demands."[2] In this arrangement, the *Diction-ary* summarizes the traits, training, and abilities required and lists the occupations which share these characteristics. In all, there are presented 114 worker trait groups, arranged into 22 "areas of work," shown below.

> Art
> Business Relations (Administration, Negotiation,
>   Consulting, Accounting, etc.)
> Clerical Work
> Counseling, Guidance, and Social Work
> Crafts (Very Broad)
> Education and Training
> Elemental Work (Signaling, Feeding Offbearing,
>   Handling)
> Engineering
> Entertainment
> Farming, Fishing, and Forestry
> Investigating, Inspecting, and Testing
> Law and Law Enforcement
> Machine Work
> Management and Supervisory Work
> Mathematics and Sciences
> Medicine and Health
> Merchandising
> Music
> Personal Services
> Photography and Communications
> Transportation
> Writing

These areas of work, and the specific worker traits groups within them, should primarily be of use in the placement functions of USES. A brief descrip-tion of work performed accompanies each of the worker trait groups, covering

[a]After all, harvesters of other crops are not excluded from group 4, and this exception does not appear to make much sense.

tools, materials, judgement, and customary location of the workingplace. This is followed by a summary of worker requirements in terms of aptitudes, attitudes, temperament, and performance. "Clues for Relating Applicants and Requirements" (such as expressed preferences, hobbies, previous successful interests and work by the applicant) and some indications of the routes whereby the jobs are entered, complete the verbal materials on each worker traits group. Associated with each of these groups, as indeed, with most of the distinct defined occupations, are codes relating to education, training, and the requirements imposed by the job.[3]

The majority of the twenty-two areas of work listed above are similar in name to the "job families" elsewhere developed by this author. This similarity arises from the fact that wherever jobs are grouped together according to the technological foci of jobs (and the promotion ladders and patterns of worker substitutability or transferability which stem from the technical nature of jobs), such groupings will include jobs making highly similar demands upon workers. When, as with the *DOT*, one starts from the alternative conceptual basis, pulling together jobs with similar worker traits characteristics, it is reasonable that the end product should be classifications that look like job families. However, it should be firmly borne in mind that the conceptual principles of classification were radically different. In one case, the focus was upon the relationship among jobs; in the other, with the nature of requirements imposed upon the human occupants of these jobs.

Data, People, and Things (DPT)

Returning to a significant aspect of the occupational group classification discussed earlier, we must consider the full content of the six digit coding scheme employed. As indicated in Table 2-1, the first three digits depict in increasing detail the occupational group to which the job belongs. The last three digits, new in the third edition of the *Dictionary*, attempt to provide some information on the functional content of the various occupations.

In particular, an effort has been made to assess the degree of involvement of various jobs with "data, people, and things." It is argued that estimates of the importance of these three "functions" reveal the "total level of complexity" of the job.[4] It should be noted that this idea is not one that has never been tried. When confronted with massive placement needs for discharged veterans after World War II, the British Ministry of Labour developed a similar coding system. Nonetheless, it is a departure for the *Dictionary*, and deserves close examination.

The method employed is to describe the level of involvement with each of the three functions by means of a hierarchy of verbs indicating what the worker "does to" data, people, and things. As the *Dictionary* admits, the arrangement of verbs for People "is somewhat arbitrary and can be considered a hierarchy only in the most general sense."[5] The arrangement for "data" will serve as an example to clarify the method used, while suggesting that the *DOT*'s reservations about the "people" hierarchy should not be restricted to it alone.

The following list shows the hierarchical arrangement of the possible relationships with "data":

0	Synthesizing
1	Coordinating
2	Analyzing
3	Compiling
4	Computing
5	Copying
6	Comparing
7) 8)	No Significant Relationship

The exact meanings of these summary verbs are defined in the *Dictionary*[6] and need not be reproduced at this point. More to the point is the observation, for example, that functional "levels" 4, 5, and 6 are more representative of different *types* of work than of *levels*. Level 4 involves arithmetic functions, while level 5 is basically concerned with clerical and posting duties. Level 6, however, is the most slippery since it embraces "judging the readily observable functions, structural or compositional characteristics (whether similar to or divergent from obvious standards) of data, people, or things."[7] This standard would clearly include many low-level testing and inspection jobs. In a sense, what we see here is a "hierarchy," which, in the final analysis reflects the lowest-skilled data relationship for three different kinds of jobs. Whether a skill or promotion hierarchy exists (or has been accurately laid down), becomes irrelevant in a case like this.

Similar objections can be raised to the sets of verbs for People and Things. Nonetheless, we should go to the core of the problem at some point, so we will pass these by. The principal questions to be raised are: (1) Are the Data, People, and Things "functions" really adequate for describing the functioning of workers on jobs? and (2) Is there an alternative set of job dimensions which might be more valuable for placement as well as for other concerns?

In response to the first question, it would seem to be the case that, particularly for the functioning of work groups, the DPT scheme cannot work. Responsibility, especially in regard to the safety and productivity of other workers, is completely omitted. It is, generally speaking, impossible to analyze the content of such jobs in a vacuum, and when the People dimension is so arid, devoid of indications of nonmechanical human contact, the system will be of little use. Moreover, the interactions between the three DPT dimensions are likely to be important, and will not be reflected in the scheme.

Turning to the second question, the author has argued elsewhere that the characteristics of *jobs* will not be most fruitfully reflected by the DPT.[8] For nonplacement purposes (e.g. the analytical concerns of economists), information of a "job-evaluation" type is likely to be more valuable. The same observation applies to the interests, temperaments, and aptitudes data, which apply mostly to *workers* and less to *jobs*. While the latter information may be desirable from a placement viewpoint, the issue is less clear for DPT. There was some interest in the Employment Service a few years ago in the development of a set of tests which could be given to applicants, the results of which would indicate a worker's profile vis à vis DPT. Thus, workers' and jobs' DPT characteristics could be matched in the placement functioning of the Employment Service. If DPT have been found less useful in placement than other sorts of information (as evidenced by abandonment of the test project), the scheme may not be worth perpetuation.

Finally, let us explore one possible application of the DPT characteristics, which was part of the earlier British experiment, and has been employed extensively by Sidney A. Fine.[9] This area of research centers upon the use of the DPT scales to indicate, not only the level of involvement with the three functions, but the relative orientation of the job as well. In brief, can one take a meaningful look at the nature of jobs by comparing the portion of them devoted to Data, People, and Things, respectively? In practice, the 0 to 8 coding scales have been reversed (so that 8 is used to reflect highest involvement), summed, and then the proportion of the sum used to indicate orientation of jobs.

For example, certain industrial power engineers are coded 1-5-1 on DPT scales. If the numbers are reversed, the levels become 7-3-7. One then would be tempted to say that this job is (roughly) 41% data, 18% people, and 41% things. Whether or not such comparisons can be made between different jobs, it should at least be possible to compare the orientation of the same job as it is affected by technological change.

The difficulties with this approach have been discussed elsewhere.[10] In general, there is no assurance that any of the three scales are linear, or that they are comparable in their scaling. Moreover, as indicated, any problems within the hierarchical coding itself would ruin such measures of orientation. We have seen some problems in the data-verb classification, and the *Dictionary* admits its shortcomings for People. The decision of the BES to leave the orientation material out of the *DOT* seems to have been a wise one.

Training Times

In view of the fact that the *Dictionary* provides our only source of estimates for education and training times on a universal basis, a few comments are required. The *DOT*'s 1966 Supplement presents for each occupation estimates of required levels of "general educational development" and "specific vocational preparation." The former category "embraces ... [formal and informal education]

which contributes to the worker's (a) reasoning development and ability to follow instructions and (b) acquisition of 'tool' knowledges, such as language and
mathematical skills." Specific Vocational Preparation estimates reflect the
"amount of time required to learn the techniques, acquire information and
develop the facility needed for average performance in a specific job-worker
situation."[11]

Several criticisms must be leveled against these training time estimates, indicating conceptual problems and practical pitfalls to be avoided in the future. In
order for the GED estimates—which clearly bear some relationship to formal
schooling—to be useful for educational planning, they must be given year-equivalents. As the BES did not believe this to be proper or possible, Eckaus and the
present author finally yielded to the temptation.[12] In the latter case, application
of the Eckaus year-equivalents to GED levels produced serious questions about
the quality of the estimates themselves: 47% of the 3-digit census groups pos-
sessed lower median schooling attainment in 1960 than the estimated requirements. Sidney Fine has suggested a number of problems with this finding, due in
some part to possible errors or misclassifications of *DOT* jobs to census
groups.[13] Be that as it may, economists, educators, and planners are still likely
to want data on year-equivalents, and as yet, adequate data do not exist.[14]

SVP has problems of its own, stemming basically from the inseparable nature
of many chunks of on-the-job training. Thus, OJT for one job in a well-defined
progression ladder is also "relevant OJT" for the next one above it. Whether this
period of time is counted once or twice or at all by the *DOT* estimates is very
unclear. Whether the overall picture of the training pattern pertaining to the
specific jobs in the cluster which surrounds them can be understood in the *DOT*
framework is rather doubtful.

Census

The summary classifications of the United States Census of Population are the
most widely used framework for occupational analysis. They have been used by
academic economists when considering types of work performed, technological
change, labor force status, and structural unemployment. Other social scientists
have employed these data for studies of the social-economic status of occupations, for analysis of the determinants of such status, and to assess class differences in education, marriage and divorce, political views and voting patterns. The
major census groups also comprise the vehicle for most current employment
information. In the Current Population Survey, some two dozen detailed occupations are reported, but for state and regional data, primary reliance is placed
upon the major groups laid out by the census. Thus, for a variety of reasons, it is
essential to take a deep look at the principles and practical applications which
these numbers reflect.

At this point, the structure of census occupational information may be briefly outlined. The most visible parts are the major groupings, which vary in number presented according to the detail desired for the particular table. In general, there are the following major groups—professional, managerial, clerical, sales, craftsman, operatives, laborers, service workers, farmers, and farm laborers. Within these classes are grouped nearly three-hundred distinct occupations, some further subdivided by industry (e.g., the "not elsewhere classified" portions of foremen, laborers, operatives, etc.). The detailed occupations within these classes are not defined by a description of tasks, duties, and requirements, but in terms of a very long list[15] containing all the responses from the census form which have been allocated to the various detailed titles. Such theory as has grown up regarding principles of classification is largely aimed at the major groups; their real meaning must, however, be obtained by going through the coding manual.

The census occupational classification system was developed over a period of some sixty years, in a series of sporadic efforts by economists, sociologists and census takers. The focal interest of the classification did, however, remain remarkedly constant—the measurement of the importance of various social and economic classes in the United States. The demonstration of social progress and the advancement of the laboring classes was a primary motivation for the development of these measures. Karl Marx had not been alone in predicting the dilution, displacement, and exploitation of labor. With the best American credentials—Civil War general, commissioner of the census, president of M.I.T., first president of the American Economic Association—Francis Amasa Walker exhorted the working class to vigilance in face of the constant threat of "industrial degradation." These questions may not seem most pressing today, but the occupational classes of the census are in large part descended from that line of inquiry.

Passing over considerable quantities of historical information,[16] the most recent exposition of the purposes and goals of the census classification was given in 1943. Alba M. Edwards, who should be remembered as the long-time observer of the nation's occupational status, summed up the introduction to his final work in these words:

In the analysis of many of the problems which concern workers as people, and not merely as productive machines, as well as in the analysis of social and economic problems generally, there is, and long has been, a real need for statistics showing in summary form an occupational distribution of the nation's labor force—a need for statistics that cut across industry lines and bring together into one occupationally homogenous group *all of the workers belonging to the same social economic class, with but minor regard to the occupations they pursue* or to the particular part of the industrial field in which they work.[17]

To readers of the present study, Edwards' statement is remarkable on three major counts. In the first place, it is now almost three decades since the goals and principles of census classification were spelled out and thus brought to the attention of users of the data. Second, the emphasis on social and economic status is clearly indicated—we must remember that such classifications are likely to be inappropriate for some uses to which they have been put. Finally, one can quarrel with the social-economic class homogeneity of the resulting data to a considerable degree.

It is my feeling that the first point is crucial to an understanding of the others. In the absence of a clear statement of the conceptual foundations of the major census groups, there is no means by which analytical users of the data have their attention called to the nature of the classification that they are utilizing. Similarly, the need to live within the boundaries of Edwards' principles would tend to keep these groups homogenous when census personnel alter classifications. Alternatively, they might recognize the need for a classification framework based upon different concepts.

Without belaboring points which have been made elsewhere,[18] we may briefly indicate the importance of these problems. Possibly, the most questionable application of the social-economic groups by economists has been in the area of labor market efficiency, and particularly in the analysis of "structural unemployment."[19] We may leave aside the theoretical objection that a model of perfect competition is somewhat inappropriate as a bench mark for measuring or theorizing about the structure of unemployment in a world filled with internal job ladders and seniority-based promotion/layoff systems. More to the present point is the fact that the census groupings do not embrace unified groups of *jobs* (measure of work performed) which one might be concerned about from the demand side of the market and from the standpoint of technological change. Nor, it should be emphasized, are they measures of supply side characteristics: in particular, groupings of people with similar skills who are perhaps being left behind by more rapid demand shifts. These summary census measures are not satisfactory classifications for such purposes—nor were they intended to be.

With respect to the lack of social-economic homogeneity in the current classifications, it should be said that this is one of the few problems in the whole area of occupational classification which seems capable of generating mirth in the general population. Serious commentators have been distressed by bank presidents and prostitutes appearing in the same broad class, lion tamers grouped with wine tasters, and so on. Several years ago, a national Sunday supplement amused its readers with the revelation that bank robbers are professional, etc., workers. I believe that I owe the following counter-suggestion to James Duesenberry, that the latter be classed as "non-bank financial intermediaries."

Despite the humor which can be extracted from the situation, there are real, serious problems with the major census groups from the viewpoint of homogeneity. No one analyzing skills, jobs, or the structure of unemployment should be interpreting the current "Sales" group as meaningful: newsboys and peddlers (244,992 employed in 1960) are grouped with stockbrokers and insurance salesmen (393,174 in 1960). There are serious problems in the "Professional, Technical and Kindred Workers" class as well. Instructive in this instance is a brief review of the process whereby the situation came about. The 1940 census showed two groups in this area: professional and semiprofessional workers. Among the latter were nurses, miscellaneous entertainers, and airplane pilots. One of the difficulties with social-economic classifications of this nature is that these groups (and their representatives) took affront. Through various forms of persuasion, by 1950 all these groups had advanced to full professional status. A social-economic classification, like Marx's capitalism, may contain within itself the seeds of its own destruction.

There is certainly nothing conceptually wrong with a classification of the population which reflects social and economic class. For a variety of users and problems, it is clearly what is required. Nonetheless, if the census intends to retain—for purposes of historical comparability, say—something close to the current system, it should: (1) clearly specify in the 1970 volumes the nature of the classification and the goals to which it is addressed and (2) make a serious effort to ensure that the actual groups and occupations reflect the announced purpose.

The International Standard Classification of Occupations (ISCO)

The International Labour Office, working with the International Conference of Labour Statisticians, has attempted to develop an internationally applicable system for occupational information. The document which presents the results, *The International Standard Classification of Occupations*, was developed in three stages from 1949 to 1957, and published in 1958.[20] In recent years, work has been underway on a second edition which was published in 1969, dated 1968.

The purposes for which ISCO was developed may be briefly summarized: "(a) to facilitate international comparisons of statistical data originating at the national level, (b) to give guidance to governments wishing to develop or revise national occupational classification systems; and (c) to serve as a means of identifying specific national occupations of international interest."[21]

The historical development of ISCO is somewhat different than that lying behind most national systems of occupational information. Customarily, aggregate occupational information has not been developed with a view towards usefulness in day-to-day manpower operations. By way of example, the different end uses of *DOT* and census information in the United States explain a number of the variations between the two systems. ISCO, however, had as its direct parent an earlier classification system aimed directly at facilitating particular manpower adjustments. The *International Classification of Occupations for Migration and Employment Placement* (published in 1952) was developed by ILO and OECD to assist in the matching of jobs and workers in postwar Europe as well as to improve job information for longer range migration from Europe.

That ISCO had in its background some operating value in microeconomic labor market operations should not be construed as evidence that it has successfully resolved the conflict which exists in the United States between the two types of data. On the one hand, its claim of comprehensiveness is a qualified one—"all occupations in the world are covered *although not all are mentioned by specific title*."[22] The criterion for inclusion of an occupational title is the international numerical or technical importance of the occupation, rather than the national standards of importance which would be applied by individual countries. Moreover, it is recognized that "the segment of work called an 'occupation' " involves a range of duties and tasks associated with relatively broad areas of work performed.[23] Very seldom is there any pretense that particular concrete jobs are being described. The classification is therefore a rather general one—a survey of its contents will reveal that its usefulness lies more on the side of census-type information than in potential value for employment services or labor exchanges in industrialized nations.

The ISCO Groups

The 1958 version of ISCO recognized ten major groups of occupations covering civilian employment. It may be of interest to list them at this point, since such internationally comparable figures as are now published are limited to these groups.

0. Professional, Technical and Related Workers
1. Administrative, Executive, & Managerial Workers
2. Clerical Workers
3. Sales Workers
4. Farmers, Fishermen, Hunters, Loggers & Related Workers
5. Miners, Quarrymen and Related Workers
6. Workers in Transportation and Communications Occupations
7/8. Craftsmen, Production Process Workers and Laborers,
     not elsewhere classified
9. Service, Sport and Recreation Workers
X. Workers not classifiable by occupation

The listing above is generally similar to that of the U.S. census. The principal differences arise in the lumping of craftsmen, "operatives," and laborers into a single major group and the use of two quasi-industrial groups: miners and transport-communications workers.

Beneath these major groups lie 73 minor groups, divided into 201 unit groups, which are broken into 1,345 occupations. Unlike the U.S. Census Bureau's occupations, ISCO contains definitions for each of the titles, attempting to describe each of the occupations in terms of the work performed: general functions and duties, principal tools and materials, indications of possible variations among the discrete jobs within the occupation.[24]

Inasmuch as the fundamental principle upon which ISCO was based was that of "work performed," exception could be taken to both the "industrial" groups and the broad blue-collar group. Both groups—although for different reasons—cover broad ranges and different generic types of work performed. In view of this fact, the 1965 ISCO Working Group proposed that the miners and transport-communications groups be abolished for the second edition. Their component jobs would be redistributed among the other groups, mostly to a new blue-collar major group. Of the thirteen minor groups which were placed in major groups 5 and 6 in 1958, ten would be reallocated to the blue-collar group, two (ship's officers and airline pilots) to the professional category, and one (postmen and messengers) would be assigned to the clerical area.[25]

For a variety of reasons, the ILO did not feel that the broad blue-collar group (7/8 above) could be broken down to more homogeneous major groups based upon skill. A change in title was proposed ("Crafts, Production Process and Operating Occupation"), but creation of new major groups based upon skill, type of work, or stage in the production process was rejected. In the ILO's opinion, "the purposes of (the work being carried out) are broadly similar." Differences in technology are viewed as principal determinants of the skill levels and the distributions between craftsmen, operatives, and laborers at various skill levels in the different countries.[26] In view of the current interest in just such questions, it is unfortunate that the revised ISCO did not give a stronger impetus toward obtaining the relevant data.

The principles and structure of the 1968 edition are roughly similar to that of 1958, with the exception of the absorption of the industrial groups into other classes. In view of the fact that the new edition is intended to serve as a basis for the 1970 round of national censuses, it is desirable to lay out the major groups which will probably be the form which the vast majority of internationally comparable data will take. The major groups are now eight in number:

0/1   Professional, Technical and Related Workers
2   Administrative and Managerial Workers
3   Clerical and Related Workers
4   Sales Workers
5   Service Workers
6   Agricultural, Animal Husbandry, and Forestry Workers
7/8/9 Production and Related Workers, Transport Equipment
          Operators and Laborers

Although the number of major groups has been reduced (by the amalgamation of old groups 5 and 6 into new group 7/8/9), detail at finer levels has been increased: 83 minor groups, 284 unit groups, and 1,506 detailed occupations. This latter number reflects a 12% increase over the 1958 volume.

Utilization of ISCO

The ILO is rather vague on the extent of utilization of ISCO, with examples in the published volumes being limited to general potentialities instead of descriptions of specific instances of use. In response to a question by the author, concerning how many countries use ISCO for their occupational statistics, the International Labour Office replied that, as a general rule, individual countries do not use occupational classifications identical with ISCO. The great majority of countries, however, have made adaptations of their national occupational classifications, or developed new classifications in order to be able to report data in conformity with the international standard. Furthermore, the ILO went on, while up-to-date information was lacking, it was known (in 1967) that some 80 countries have used ISCO directly or indirectly for one or more purposes, including use in connection with censuses, employment placement and other applications, as well as for purposes of adjusting, revising or developing national classifications.[27]

The 1967 edition of the *Yearbook of Labour Statistics* (published by the ILO) presents employment figures by ISCO major groups for 99 countries and dependencies (its table 2B). Some of this comparability reflects actual use of ISCO by individual nations; some comes from reclassification of their own figures to an ISCO basis, either in the statistical office of the country or by the Statistical Branch of the ILO.

Two major difficulties in using these data should be mentioned, although this goes a bit out of the narrow path this data review follows in general. Academic and governmental researchers have made and will continue to make use of these figures as a source of international comparisons of employment structure. Thus two brief notes of caution are in order.

First, under the circumstances, uniform application by diverse government agencies of the agreed-upon definitions is highly unlikely. This difficulty is probably most pronounced in the estimates given for group 4—farmers, etc. Particularly in the less developed countries the status of rural women and children is hard to assess consistently. The lines between employment, unemployment, and out of labor force—never very clear—become even fuzzier when the concept of "economically active" is applied to such sectors of the population. As the *Yearbook* itself puts it, "the practice varies between countries as regards the treatment of . . . seasonal workers and persons engaged in part-time economic activities."[28]

The importance of intercountry variations in practice can be suggested dramatically by a pair of observations for a single country. In 1960, the economically active population of Syria in farming pursuits was given as 459,000 males, 38,000 females, or 48.3% of the total. In 1966, the same country shows 57.8% of its total labor force in major group 4: 520,000 males and 318,000 females. Forewarned is forearmed.

Secondly, in any such document, the attempts to convert from one set of classifications to another are hazardous undertakings from a strictly mechanical standpoint. The collection, definition, and publication of employment figures are performed as scrupulously in the United States as in most countries, but the *Yearbook* shows the proportion of "blue-collar workers" (group 7/8) falling from 31.4 to 17.3% from 1960 to 1966, while miners and transport-communications workers (total of groups 5 and 6) rose from 5.1 to 18.1%. Where the problem arose is of little concern to the present inquiry, but should serve as a warning to those—like the present author on an earlier occasion—who might be tempted to use these figures without extreme caution.

Improving Social Economic Measures

The Edwardsian Census classification was based upon the social-economic characteristics of the employed population; despite practical failings in application, this remains the underlying principle. It will be argued in following sections that such a system may not be the most fruitful or conceptually sound starting point for analysis of work performance and the workers performing it. Nevertheless, attention should be given to recent efforts to improve social-economic classification techniques, if only because of the number of such attempts.

Starting from a minor disagreement with one of the author's earlier discussions of this subject, Jerome Gordon has set forth an alternative approach towards improved occupational groups.[29] The alternative proposed is to construct a system which more accurately reflects social and economic status measures. With such a purpose, there can be no quarrel. If distributions of the work force by indices of social-economic status are desirable (and for many purposes they are), then they should be done correctly.[30]

Gordon proposed a classification which would reflect social-economic characteristics on the one hand, and on the other, the "modern-traditional" distinction earlier proposed by Jaffe.[31] It would be pointless to summarize all of Gordon's procedures; let it suffice to say that census SES rankings[32] were transmuted into estimates of the relative levels of social economic status. These were then used to form new occupational groups: a line of demarcation was drawn between groups when "second differences were zero" on the list of values. By these techniques, fourteen major occupational groups (plus two for farmers and farm workers whose SES values were not estimated by census) could be distinguished. The evaluated occupations were then allocated to six Jaffe-Froomkin[33] "Major Livelihood Code Groups," producing the matrix shown in Table 2-2.

Table 2-2

Cross-Classification of Major Occupational Groups Based on Relative Values of Socio-Economic Status (SES) Scores and Major "Livelihood" Codes Employed Males (000), 1960

		Major Livelihood Code Groups						
Group #	SES Score Range	Modern[a]	Classical[b]	Managerial, Administrative & Distribution[c]	Service[d]	Industrial & Commercial, Unskilled[e]	Forestry, Fisheries & Agriculture[f]	Occupation Not Reported[g]
1	96-100	1,238.1	343.9	365.4	—	—	—	—
2	90- 95	808.1	107.4	1,670.4	—	—	—	—
3	81- 89	748.9	707.7	2,776.2	—	—	—	—
4	76- 80	1,588.1	—	898.4	—	—	—	—
5	71- 75	1,391.8	82.6	2,355.0	368.0	—	—	—
6	64- 70	1,429.5	250.5	383.3	37.7	—	—	—
7	56- 63	4,227.9	254.4	1,678.7	28.3	13.2	—	—
8	49- 55	1,601.6	244.7	205.4	0.2	15.6	—	—
9	40- 48	2,913.5	282.4	81.4	224.1	77.7	—	—
10	31- 39	1,244.5	1,399.0	3.8	896.5	251.7	—	1,987.0
11	25- 30	230.8	—	—	104.4	795.3	—	—
12	20- 24	10.2	43.6	182.1	—	254.2	—	—
13	14- 19	260.6	7.0	—	939.4	919.5	193.4	—
14	1- 13	192.4	—	22.7	61.3	325.5	151.9	—
15	Farmers	—	—	—	—	—	2,387.6	—
16	Farm Workers	—	—	—	—	—	1,201.8	—
Total		17,886.0	3,723.2	10,622.8	2,659.9	2,652.7	3,934.7	1,987.0

aModern occupations are Census Occupation Codes 100 for Professionals, 400 and 410 for Craftsmen, and 600 for Operatives.

bClassical occupations are Census Occupation Codes 200 and 210 for Professionals, 500 for Craftsmen, and 610 for Operatives.

cManagerial, Administrative and Distribution occupations are Census Occupation Codes 230 and 240 for Managers, 300 and 310 for Clericals, and 330 for Sales Workers.

dService occupations are Census Occupation Codes 800 for Private Household Service Workers, and 810 for Service Workers.

eIndustrial and Commercial Unskilled occupations are Census Occupation Code 902 for Laborers.

fForestry, Fisheries and Agricultural occupations are Census Occupation Codes 220 for Farmers and Farm Managers, 900 for Farm Workers, and 901 for Laborers.

gOccupations not reported are Census Occupation Code 995.

Sources: U.S. Bureau of the Census, U.S. Census of Population: 1960. Detailed Characteristics. U.S. Summary. Final Report PC(1)-1D.
U.S. Government Printing Office, Washington, D.C. table 202, pp. 1-522-29.
Unpublished Jaffe "livelihood" codes for the 1960 U.S. census listing of detailed occupations.

Reproduced from Gordon, "Occupational Classifications: Current Issues and an Interim Solution," *Proceedings of the American Statistical Association*, 1967, Social Statistics Section, p. 282, by permission of the American Statistical Association.

One of the most important features of a classification with this theoretical basis is to circumvent a number of problems associated with other proposed changes in census data. In particular, such an aggregation format claims immunity to problems of historical comparability associated with changes in the detailed data gathered.[34] Thus, once a set of SES value groups has been set up correctly, thereby rectifying distortions in the current census groupings, it is possible to subdivide and redefine occupations without greatly jeopardizing comparability with previous or succeeding censuses. In brief, relative SES levels will describe the same things at all times.

There would, of course, be some qualification to the foregoing generalization, as Gordon is aware. On the one side, as the massive groupings of disparate jobs bundled together in the "not elsewhere classified" categories are broken up, there will be some diffusion of their components among SES levels. To the extent that n.e.c. groups include jobs with differing status (much as they now incorporate jobs with varying skill, job content, and technological characteristics), some problems of comparability would arise.

In the second place, the question remains unanswered about the desirability of assigning primacy to social and economic status in generating a framework for occupational data. The relative social-economic status of various occupations changes over time, often for reasons that we can understand by good old supply and demand in the labor market. Thus, we by no means have an "invariable standard of value" by which to assess the progress of society. For this reason alone it would seem unwise to build up an entire system of occupational information solely to measure the groupings which Gordon has outlined. It should be emphasized that this was not his point, but this leads us to the following problem: will there be a conflict between the detailed data found desirable from economic and technical points of view and the desire to assess social-economic status levels from those data?

It would be constructive for any detailed information to avoid what Richard Stone has called the "Procrustean approach"—a "single classification . . . (applied) everywhere whether it is suitable or not."[35] If our atom of information is to be the job, with correlative information on the technology in which it is embedded, will this prevent the attachment of SES values and assignment to the appropriate groups? The answer, naturally enough, depends upon the relationships between the concepts "job" and "occupation." From this point of view, a common sociological definition poses no problems:

The specific kind of work a person does in a socially evaluated work situation generally is thought of as a *job*, while an *occupation* refers to the characteristics that are transferable among employers.[36]

Moreover, sociologists and psychologists of varying stripe have analyzed the status relations that obtain among occupations in the outside world, and among jobholders inside the enterprise. Thus, there would seem to be no necessary incompatibility between job-based data collection and aggregation to meaningful occupational groups—meaningful, say, in the sense that field survey research can be done on occupational prestige and status.[37] The task for sociologists would be to build up the atomistic data into structures useful to them. These structures are not likely to be the same as those desired by various groups of economists, educational planners, or vocational counselors.

Classes Related to Worker Interests

Occupational and industrial psychologists are often concerned with the relationship between the interests of workers and the nature of the job. Such relationships, the manner in which work interests are formed, and workers' perceptions of the features of various jobs are clearly relevant to analysis of occupational choice, mobility between jobs, and worker performance.

This concern with the relationship between interests and work led Dr. Anne Roe to propose an occupational classification similar in many respects to the job content matrix discussed below. Her scheme is two-fold: groups of occupations based upon the primary focus of the work, and *levels* defined by differences in "personal autonomy and the level of skill and training required."[38] The application of these principles yields the matrix of table 2-3.

Two points should be made about this matrix. As can be seen, use of a psychological or worker interest basis for assessing primary focus leads to a number of differences from the classification that would arise based upon the technical focus of the job. For example, miners' work is much the same as many of Roe's "Technology" occupations, but from the viewpoint of interest, the "outdoor" nature of the work is overriding. In this case, "outdoor" is a shorthand for what economists might term primary occupations—those concerned with agricultural and extractive work. Thus, bulldozer operators, whose work is definitely outdoor, appear under the very broad group, "Technology."

In the second place, the interest classification includes in any grouping a wide variety of technically defined work foci. Both taxi drivers and waiters indeed provide services, but they work within highly different technologies. The service aspect may be most important for placement and satisfaction in the light of workers' interests and preferences, but the content of the jobs differs sharply. Nonetheless, the point should be stressed that any set of detailed occupational data which fits a job content matrix would seem to be amenable to classification by the Roe schema.

Job Content Classifications

A final form of data aggregation has been proposed in earlier work of the present author.[39] This method of classification is closely related to the analytical frame-

Table 2-3
Roe's Two-Way Classification of Occupations

Level	Service	Business Contact	Organization	Technology	Outdoor	Science	General Cultural	Arts and Entertainment
								Group
1	Personal therapists Social work supervisors Counselors	Promoters	United States President and Cabinet officers Industrial tycoons International bankers	Inventive geniuses Consulting or chief engineers Ships' commanders	Consulting specialists	Research scientists University, college faculties Medical specialists Museum curators	Supreme Court Justices University, college faculties Prophets Scholars	Creative artists Performers, great Teachers, university equivalent Museum curators
2	Social workers Occupational therapists Probation, truant officers (with training)	Promoters Public relations counselors	Certified public accountants Business and government executives Union officials Brokers, average	Applied scientists Factory managers Ships' officers Engineers	Applied scientists Landowners and operators, large Landscape architects	Scientists, semi-independent Nurses Pharmacists Veterinarians	Editors Teachers, high school and elementary	Athletes Art critics Designers Music arrangers
3	YMCA officials Detectives, police sergeants Welfare workers City inspectors	Salesmen: auto, bond, insurance, etc. Dealers, retail and wholesale Confidence men	Accountants, average Employment managers Owners, catering, dry-cleaning, etc.	Aviators Contractors Foremen (DOT I) Radio operators	County agents Farm owners Forest rangers Fish, game wardens	Technicians, medical, X-ray, museum Weather observers Chiropractors	Justices of the Peace Radio announcers Librarians	Ad writers Designers Interior decorators Showmen
4	Barbers Chefs Practical nurses Policemen	Auctioneers Buyers (DOT I) House canvassers Interviewers, poll	Cashiers Clerks, credit, express, etc. Foremen, warehouse Salesclerks	Blacksmiths Electricians Foremen (DOT II) Mechanics, average	Laboratory testers, dairy products, etc. Miners Oil well drillers	Technical assistants	Law clerks	Advertising artists Decorators, window, etc. Photographers Racing car drivers
5	Taxi drivers General houseworkers Waiters City firemen	Peddlers	Clerks, file, stock, etc. Notaries Runners Typists	Bulldozer operators Deliverymen Smelter workers Truck drivers	Gardeners Farm tenants Teamsters, cowpunchers Miner's helpers	Veterinary hospital attendants		Illustrators, greeting cards Showcard writers Stagehands
6	Chambermaids Hospital attendants Elevator operators Watchmen		Messenger boys	Helpers Laborers Wrappers Yardmen	Dairy hands Farm laborers Lumberjacks	Nontechnical helpers in scientific organization		

Reprinted with permission from Anne Roe, *The Psychology of Occupations* copyright ©1956, John Wiley and Sons, Inc.

work for analysis of job and training breadth developed in Part 2 below. The principle of classification by job content is based upon two facets of the jobs in any economy: (a) the technical, material, or functional focus of the job (which determines *job family*); and (b) the level of job content—skill, responsibility, etc. —which is involved.

At the enterprise level, the existence of job families containing jobs of varying complexity is well-known. These jobs may be centered around a piece of equipment: a rolling mill or a locomotive, or around a functional department: billing office, or personnel division.[40] In these clusters of jobs, hierarchies of skill and responsibility are apparent:

Locomotive	Billing Office
engineer	manager
fireman	assistant managers
brakeman	chief clerks
	bill posters, key punchers, etc.

These clusters and rankings are important for adequate understanding of a wide variety of labor market phenomena. Promotion and transfer patterns, wage structures, and the nature of on-the-job training and prejob training requirements are quite obviously involved. Improved models of wage determination must recognize that wages and employment in these grouped jobs tend to move together, as they are (broadly speaking) all affected by the same forces.

Moving from the level of the individual plant or enterprise, analogous job family and content level concepts can fruitfully be applied to the whole structure of employment. In brief, the proposals made in *Job Content* lead to a matrix of the type shown in table 2-4.

In such an array of the work performed in the economy, similar jobs appear in the various cells. Thus, in the job family entitled "Health," all kinds of physicians and surgeons appear at the highest content level, with technicians and nurses falling lower, with attendants and aides of diverse sorts at the bottom of the pile.[41] The following characteristics should be reflected by such a classification:

1. Wages in a job family should tend to move together.
2. "Promotions" in the aggregate sense of upward mobility should tend to be concentrated within the family ladders.
3. "Transfers" in an aggregate sense should be most common within cells or between cells at the lowest levels of job content.
4. The technical nature and content (as well as the level) of training and education are partially specified by the job family's technical or functional focus, and partly by level of job in the family.

Thus, a classification of this nature adds one important factor to the elasticities stipulated by Cain, Hansen, and Weisbrod, a factor antecedent, in fact, to the conditions they desire. Job families broken down by levels of job content—in other words, a technological classification—will result in classifications of workers which will have higher elasticities of substitution and cross-elasticities of supply within their groups than between them.[42] Further, the information about both supply and demand sides of a labor market supplied by a job content framework will be substantially in excess of that which would arise from direct application of their criteria. Most significantly, the job vacancy data recommended by the President's Committee to Appraise Employment and Unemployment Statistics are only comprehensible in such a framework, despite the current collection of such data without it.

The Quest for a Standard Occupational Classification

The era of detailed study of labor markets and employment patterns began, for all practical purposes, in the 1930s. Parallel with these concerns grew up an interest in the classification systems used to describe employment and occupational distributions. The first task to be undertaken was the development of a standard industrial classification, the result of cooperation among the various producers and consumers of industrial statistics.

The natural next step seemed to be in the direction of a standard occupational classification. To this end a committee of concerned users and creators of occupational data was established in 1938. The committee addressed itself to the problem of the diverse kinds of occupational data in existence—census, BLS wage surveys, BES and USES records being the most important.

In the committee's view, the problems associated with bringing the various parts of the occupational picture together were due to differences in the way the two classes of respondents perceived the employment relationship. In brief," the employee describes himself as a worker, and the employer describes the work as a job assignment."[43] The relative ease with which the SIC was developed was attributed to the existence of a single source of information in this area: employers.[44] Although this is a fair summary of the impediments to reconciliation of two existing types of information, there is no obvious reason why new data could not be collected which avoided the difficulty. It should be possible to get job assignment information from workers, even though it may be impossible to get employers to stop looking at workers as "job assignments" while conserving valuable social and economic information.

The committee considered in some detail one possible basis for a standard occupational classification. It was recognized that the BES and BLS were able to distinguish between grades of skill within general occupational groups. The con-

Table 2-4
Employment by Job Family and Job-Content Level, 1940, 1950, and 1960. (Thousands)[a]

Level	Tools		Machine and equipment		Inspection	Vehicle Operation	Farm	Sales A	Sales B
	Specialized	Nonspecialized	Specialized	Nonspecialized					
Total	1837	6304	981	4819	743	2127	8234	758	2564
	2539	8757	1229	6675	1143	2657	6706	1017	3482
	2370	9256	960	7386	1731	3097	3950	1266	4070
1	13	8	0	0	0	0	0	70	0
	25	10	0	0	0	0	0	142	0
	44	12	0	0	0	0	0	234	0
2	248	1172	99	0	585	153	37	441	0
	299	1918	144	0	919	180	35	562	0
	280	2310	172	0	1450	162	24	734	0
3	600	2052	160	313	121	1586	24	248	36
	875	3307	354	347	179	2045	17	313	57
	900	3548	404	423	239	2432	25	298	75
4	512	426	721	154	14	107	5107	0	2422
	612	574	731	208	17	109	4280	0	3307
	535	705	384	172	20	85	2486	0	3750
5	465	2645	0	4352	22	282	3066	0	105
	728	2948	0	6120	29	322	2374	0	118
	611	2682	0	6790	22	419	1415	0	245

	Clerical	Personal Services	Entertainment	Protection	Admin. & Org.	Research & Design	Education	Health	Welfare	Total
Total	4434	4436	288	462	3819	424	1116	981	241	44567
	6995	4386	386	610	5039	860	1290	1421	300	55485
	9496	5415	436	722	5607	1376	1926	2000	390	61456
1	257	0	181	0	236	344	1116	272	206	2703
	432	0	231	0	322	738	1290	313	259	3762
	555	0	294	0	411	1163	1926	361	334	5333
2	39	0	12	0	1263	80	0	99	35	4262
	45	0	16	0	1914	122	0	211	41	6405
	79	0	28	0	2907	213	0	293	56	8708
3	3886	772	30	241	2226	0	0	423	0	12718
	6022	923	43	347	2711	0	0	479	0	18017
	8096	1188	34	446	2204	0	0	690	0	21002
4	184	725	5	205	25	0	0	187	0	10794
	434	537	15	244	27	0	0	418	0	11514
	703	671	11	250	33	0	0	656	0	10461
5	68	2940	60	16	69	0	0	0	0	14091
	63	2926	82	12	66	0	0	0	0	15786
	63	3556	70	25	53	0	0	0	0	15951

aIn each triplet of numbers, the top figure refers to 1940. One reads down to 1950 and 1960 estimates.

From *The Job Content of the U.S. Economy* by James G. Scoville. Copyright 1969, McGraw-Hill, Inc. Used with permission of McGraw-Hill Book Company.

clusion of the committee was that similar information, as a matter of fact, could not be obtained from survey interviews with workers or (more commonly) members of their households. Moreover, if one is interested in the balance of supply and demand in various labor markets, gradations by narrow skill levels may not be of primary importance. Thus the committee abandoned the skill level notion in favor of measures of industrial attachment and work status.[45]

The final result of the committee's work was the development of a relatively short list of occupational titles which would hopefully serve as a means of conversion from one classification system to another, although at a fairly high level of aggregation. The convertibility list bears considerable resemblance to the detailed occupational groups found in the 1950 census. Aside from that, no data from other agencies seem to have been published in the format suggested. The BLS area and industry wage surveys have gone their own way, while conversion tables between census data and the 1965 *DOT* are only now in final stages of preparation.

Thus, there does not seem to have been a pot of gold at the end of the rainbow called "convertibility list." One may well wonder whether the same would not be true of a standard occupational classification, had one been developed. The various producers of occupational data do not share common needs or goals; and much the same diversity, as has been pointed out above, characterizes the users of such data. Far more important is the question of convertibility at the finest level of detail practicable, so that with these building blocks individuals can create systems of aggregation most compatible with the needs of a particular study or project.

Conclusions

A survey of currently available occupational data reveals disappointing contrasts with the proposals made by Gordon, Roe, and the present author. The *Dictionary of Occupational Titles* is of reduced usefulness in empirical research as it lacks estimates of employment; its "Areas of Work" are not conceptually based on technically oriented families and clusters of jobs, and there are serious difficulties with the corollary data about the defined jobs (in particular the functional level and training time estimates). Census data and their classifications are a hodgepodge of inherited concerns with social economic status and inaccurate classifications. ISCO is a step ahead in that its announced concern is with "type of work" and that its detailed titles are explicitly defined. Its 1506 specific occupations might provide a starting point for expansion of our basic census information, although the major and intermediate groups require some amendment.

In contrast, the three reforming authors have proposed systems of classification with clear conceptual bases which, if consistently applied, would yield information consonant with their goals. The implications of these studies for our occupational data base are quite straightforward: (1) we require considerably increased detail; and (2) this detail must be capable of aggregation in a variety of ways. Data which are based upon specific jobs, firmly placed in the technical context of surrounding jobs and technology, should meet these criteria. Moreover, such data provide the proper base for corollary information on training, wages, turnover, and the other variables which figure in the model of Part II.

Part 2: Jobs — Theory and Illustrations

3

The Economic Theory of Jobs

Introduction

This section of the book forms part of the development of an economic theory of work, critical to understanding the relationships between work, training, and the operation of labor markets. In this treatment we will largely ignore the question of why men work and the general satisfactions and dissatisfactions arising from various kinds of work. Furthermore, the same questions as they impinge upon the choice between work and leisure are left to one side. Instead, we shall concentrate not on *why*, but *how* do men work? What forces and circumstances establish the jobs or tasks in which abstract work takes its concrete form?

The general setting in which this model is advanced may be briefly indicated by reference to recent conceptual developments. In the discipline of economics, efforts have been made to supplant neoclassical wage theory with theories applicable to the short run and to the facts of life. Dunlop and Livernash have outlined the importance of job clusters for determination of wages in the plant. Human capital theory (exemplified by the work of Becker) attempts to explain the training which goes into a job, and to explain occupational choice. In this connection, Gitelman has anticipated some of the arguments below, but with primary emphasis on wage determination.[1] Beyond the confines of economics, other social scientists have studied the processes and perceptions whereby individuals make the choice between occupations.[2]

Recognition is taken of the fact that the characteristics of jobs affect industrial relations, wages, mobility, and a host of other factors. Dunlop includes job content as one of the determinants in the rules that arise surrounding jobs. Starting from Kerr's "Balkanization" hypothesis, the theory of labor allocation and movement within the employing unit has been laid forth by Doeringer and Piore.[3] Perhaps finally, the present author has developed a framework to measure the types and levels of jobs which exist in any economy.

This wide range of theory and research has one common aspect—it all rests upon the existence of concrete jobs. Little effort has been devoted to examination of the forces which determine the nature and distribution of jobs, upon which the basic internal and external labor market structures, industrial relations rules, and mobility patterns all depend. This chapter, then, must be viewed in the context of a common need for explanation of phenomena crucial to all the other work, that is, the determination of jobs and their interrelationships.

Concern with the kinds of work performed is not new, although it has never occupied a central position in economic thinking. With rare exceptions, economics has chosen the easy road of homogeneous factors of production. Jobs and machines—the specific forms which labor and capital take—drop out of most models. The larger part of analytical concern with the nature and consequences of work has been left to other social scientists, particularly sociologists and psychologists. Perhaps that is why we have no fully developed economic theory of jobs as the concrete vehicle of abstract work.

In the economic literature on work, one must start with Adam Smith for more than perfunctory reasons of tradition. A good deal of *The Wealth of Nations* is based upon the relationship between job specialization and labor productivity. The very first sentence of this volume is noteworthy: "The greatest improvement in the productive powers of labour, and the greater part of the skill, dexterity and judgment with which it is anywhere directed, or applied, seem to have been the effects of the division of labor."[4] The particular "art"—the industry-specific technology involved—determines the extent to which division of labor *can* be pursued; given the technology, the size of product markets determines how far it *will* be pursued.[5] Thus, job design is determinate in Smith's model.

That the division of labor might result in increasing human misery was stressed by Sismondi, who among classical economists was most firmly opposed to the consequences of mechanization. While recognizing the productivity advances involved, Sismondi is inclined "to curse the division of labor and mechanical inventions, when we see to what extent they have reduced beings who were created fellow men."[6] Indeed Adam Smith was not unaware of the same effects—"The man whose whole life is spent in performing a few simple operations . . . generally becomes as stupid and ignorant as it is possible for a human creature to become." "His dexterity at his own particular trade seems . . . to be acquired at the expense of his intellectual, social, and martial virtues.[7] Modern sociological writers (Adam Abruzzi, Georges Friedmann, Daniel Bell) have been no less critical. Unlike Smith, who argued that the state should remedy these conditions through education, these later writers have raised more fundamental questions—Is the design of job content mechanically laid down by technology? May there not be an optimum degree of division of labor independent of the extent of the market?

Such is perhaps the central focus of this essay. Those writers, like Karl Marx, who have emphasized the technological side of job creation—in conjunction with the competitive characteristics of capitalism—have only a partial picture of the whole process whereby human work is translated into specific jobs. This incomplete view derives from the general tendency to consider a narrow range of industrial examples largely drawn from the earlier periods of industrialization. As Hoffmann, Kuznets, Chenery, Rostow, and many others have pointed out, the industrial distribution of economic activity is different at various levels or stages of development. Observations of the inexorable and debilitating effects of mechanization are rooted in the historical epoch whence these observations arose. It is significant in this regard that later writers on the relationships of monotony and fatigue to the division of labor have been cognizant of the particular industrial areas to which their ideas and findings apply.

The preceding is a rough sketch of what might be called the classical approach to determination of job content. In a parallel with classical price theory, the jobs which arise are rooted in the technology of production. When one turns his attention to more recent writers, a new strain of thought is found. Among others, Lancaster[8] and Mandelbrot[9] form a neoclassical school in which the emphasis shifts to questions of occupational choice by individuals.[10] The task of this essay is to fuse the two theoretical approaches to incorporate both the supply of job types and the choices which are made regarding them by workers and managers. In the following pages, we shall develop a more general theory of the forces and conditions leading to the appearance of various types of jobs.

At this point, a sketch of the chapter's future course can be presented in conjunction with definitions of some of the terms (provisionally) employed.

The first section deals primarily with the "supply side" of the arena in which concrete jobs are created. *Technology*, defined in general as the form which non-human means of production take, determines the basic circumstances in which work is performed. *Work* is defined as the totality of labor input associated with advancing a commodity or service from one state of fabrication to another. The disaggregability of this global input measure, work, is conditioned by the technology, and results in a variety of *job options*. These latter are the various available combinations of specific *jobs* which will suffice to perform the work. Jobs themselves are defined in terms of the tasks and duties which comprise them.

The second section will look at the various factors which affect the choice among job options made by the management of an employing unit. The customary assumptions of rationality and cost-minimization are made regarding managerial preferences. In the third section, we turn our attention to the preferences of workers and/or their organizations regarding this choice, and the last section brings the two preference sets together to explore the circumstances under which various equilibrium positions will arise. Chapter 4 looks at several case studies exploring the relationship between the content of jobs and training, mobility and occupational choice, and presenting a few empirical measures of the breadth of tasks and duties associated with several jobs.

Technology and Jobs

The typical production function approach to output-effort relationships presupposes the existence of a chosen technology and an associated job structure. This may be implicit in the model, as where gross flows of labor services are the arguments of production functions, or made explicit in varying degrees of detail. Disaggregation of econometric production functions by grades of labor input or specific jobs is quite rare. On the other hand, the BLS occupational-industry matrix—a Leontief-type production function—is firmly based upon measurement of a predetermined job structure at a point in time.

The choice of particular job structures is the subject of later consideration; at this point we ask: what are the *job options* which flow from a particular form of technology? Many of the constraints upon employer and worker choices are to be found in the nature of the technology linking inputs and product.

The relatively young concept of a *job* is itself determined by technology—in that it has arisen from changes in the predominant patterns of task performance over the course of history. In economies and eras characterized by traditional agricultural systems, the labor of mankind is not designated as "jobs." The work is, to be sure, performed, yet jobs per se do not arise. The major reason for this is not hard to find—tasks are usually of a sequential, not parallel, nature, so that work performed can be largely laid out in invariant temporal cycles. First, all available labor plows; then it sows, tends, reaps, and threshes—year in and year out. Although such production processes do involve some specialization of functions, there does not grow up that stable man/work-function relationship which industrial man knows as a *job*. The crafts which exist within the agricultural economy are themselves very broad, with the highest degree of specialization reached in preindustrial eras usually confined to trainee-journeyman-master gradations.

In the first instance, the growth of industrial technology supplants and supplements the craft and service sectors of the primitive economy.[11] In place of sequential processing, the parallel nature of production activities becomes characteristic of this growing sector of the economy, and finally comes to characterize the economy as a whole. It is that fact—that activities which would have fallen at different stages of the period of production are now performed simultaneously—which generates the modern phenomenon of a "job." Work in process no longer moves from beginning to end in the same hands (individual or broadly collective, as in agriculture), but now passes from hand to hand—from job to job—as it proceeds to completion.

The Central Forms of Technology

The first step in understanding the relationship of technology to job options lies in the following broad subdivisions of technological relationships between effort and product.

1. There exists a class of means of production which we term "tools"—small, individually operated pieces of equipment which usually involve the attention of one worker. Often the operation of a single tool does not form a complete job: a man utilizes more than one of these pieces of equipment. Jobs are, however,

created which center about bundles of tools which are related to bringing a product or collection of materials-in-process to a certain stage of fabrication.

2. The second broad form of technology which influences the job options available will be denoted "machines," once again following Max Weber.[12] These machines may be large or small, with the operational definition of small begin: operated alone by only one person. In such a case, the machine defines the job, and except for its relationship to the rest of the process of production (and how the single man/single machine relationship arose) need not detain us. With respect to larger machines, however, we must discover whether there are identifiable points of conjunction between men and machines where jobs arise.

If we visualize figure 3-1 below as a machine through which materials are flowing, various areas of intersection between human effort and machine functions become apparent. As Veblen puts it: these jobs involved "workmanlike manipulation at points where the machine process engaged is incomplete."[13] Briefly the worker functions associated with this idealized machine are the following:

a. feeding the machine
b. offbearing of finished work
c. control of the machine
d. manipulation of machine and/or product-in-process

Clearly these points of interaction are not exhaustive nor mutually exclusive. They do, however, provide an idea of the types of job options which exist in a machine technology. There is apparent latitude in how they are parcelled into concrete jobs.

3. The technology generally leaves spatial, sometimes temporal, gaps between the tools and machines which characterize it. These gaps also form the natural basis of a variety of job options. Ways must be devised of supplying the machines' sites with product to be worked, with moving the product to the next site, and providing the machine with motive power.

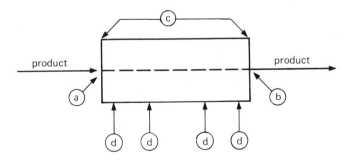

Figure 3-1. A Machine.

4. Another group of job options to be considered are those prevailing when formal and mechanical technological intervention between labor input and resulting output is not prominently involved. These technologies might broadly be characterized as "service" work, in which capital goods are not an important intermediary between effort and output. That the characteristic technological framework of this type of work is quite rudimentary implies (a) that diversity of jobs (flexibility of job options) may be greater for these areas than for other kinds of work and (b) that nontechnological factors probably control the determination of job design.

5. The last class of job options to be specified arises from human knowledge being the characteristic technology involved. In this case, a range of job options arise which are determined by the level and content of knowledge, and by the capacity of human beings to absorb, integrate, and apply it. Knowledge broadly defined is an intermediary factor of production between input and output much like a piece of physical equipment. Technological change, division of labor, and reshuffling of job options occur here as elsewhere—today's econometrician is one descendant of Adam Smith, whose "job" embraced political economy and moral philosophy.[14]

Merging of Technological Forms

The five broad types of technology developed above are not to be understood as leading to clear and separable types of job options. In fact, each technological type does produce some jobs and job options of a "pure" form, but the characteristic of most job options is to blend the various types together. In part this is due to the nature of any classification. In the strictest sense, there are probably very few "service" job options in existence which are not associated with tools, machines, or knowledge in some fashion. The bootblack, newsboy and prostitute employ certain material and technological adjuncts in various combinations. Nevertheless, these implements are not central to the service rendered. One is reminded of the adaptability in performing the core tasks revealed by Athenian prostitutes in the latter 1960s. When formal establishments were shut down by the junta, sleeping bags and street corners replaced other forms of capital goods.

The tools and machines distinction is also an arbitrary one at some point—small machines and larger tools eventually become indistinguishable. More important, however, it must be recognized that tools and machines technologies have a pattern of interrelation. The machine is typically installed, supplied, maintained, and repaired by jobs involving the primary use of tools—in some cases, use of these tools and tending the machine are combined in a single job. The point at which tool tasks are segregated from tasks incidental to running the machine depends upon the size and complexity of the two groups of tasks as compared to human mental and physical capacities.

Human knowledge as a factor of production is perhaps least often found establishing a pure type of job. Sages, prophets, and poets may approximate purity, but economists (for example) find that their work increasingly involves making complicated machines in the computer technology actually do what is desired. Leaving aside such possible complications with the "real world" of physical means of production, the basic parallelism between physical technology and human knowledge must be underscored. Knowledge, like physical capital, provides a set of job options whereby work can be accomplished. It is probable that division of labor associated with human knowledge has been at least as productive as Adam Smith ever envisioned it to be in a pin factory.

Flexibility of Job Options

That a number of job options—bundles of specific jobs—do indeed exist to carry through a quantity of work is central to the arguments that will follow. Before we can speak of the choice among job options, it needs to be shown that, in fact, more than one such bundle exists for a certain output desired. It must be shown that the apparently fixed relationship between means of production and specific jobs, which would impress itself upon observers of work in highly capitalized industries, is either illusory or a short-run phenomenon.

In the first place, there is available for the accomplishment of many kinds of work a choice between different technologies. Bhalla's note on techniques in Indian rice-milling[15] is not conclusive for heavy industry, but recent UN and ILO industry studies (for example, of chemicals and fertilizers) should satisfy needs for examples in capital intensive-industries.[16]

Second, given the work to be done and the basic technology, the literature on "job enlargement" confirms that job options do exist, that different constellations of tasks and duties incorporated in varying bundles of jobs are feasible. Tasks and duties can be reshuffled among jobs in several ways—by altering the "horizontal" time and function sequence involved, by incorporating or deleting "vertical" (supervisory and quality control) functions, by inclusion or separation of maintenance, repair and supply functions, or combinations of these adjustments.

Finally, that which appears fixed at a point in time may be quite variable in the face of options presented by continuous technological advance. The industrial engineering departments of most firms have not become so autonomous that their plans for new equipment and its manning are purely "recursive." Although some elements of technical determinism are present, managements of firms are well aware of the cost considerations involved. Our model of job design may never be in perfect equilibrium, but studies of the real world indicate that managers' reactions are in the proper direction.[17]

Employer Preferences on Job Content

Adam Smith first laid down the principle that labor productivity is a direct function of the degree of subdivision of work. The limits of division of labor were imposed by the size of the market, but beyond that the principle was unqualified. Continuing division of labor increased worker productivity in a variety of ways—increased dexterity, reduction of nonworking time on the job, and stimulation of mechanical inventions to name a few.

Jumping over a great deal of history, the scientific management movement marks the high point of practical application of Smith's principle. These engineers, of whom F.W. Taylor is the best-known writer, observed that all work could be broken into microscopic functions, which were then directly assessable in terms of the optimal time required to perform each one.[18] Critics have been somewhat unfair in evaluating this proposition, as the engineers were clearly aware that maximization of output did not entail working at top speed all day long. Scientifically arranged rest and leisure were also part of the total work package. Nonetheless, the concept that work consists basically of atomistic and additive units of motion and effort is the fundamental legacy of Adam Smith. The qualifications added by Taylorism dealt with the balance between work and rest and did not challenge the basic rule laid down.

In fact, there is very little reason to suppose that net labor productivity continues to rise as job specialization proceeds further and further. The earlier uncritical acceptance of that viewpoint, however, accounts for the counter-movement which developed in the 1920s and 1930s. The apostles of "job enlargement" found in reality that the division of labor had frequently overshot the mark—that productivity would rise if jobs were broadened. The examples they brought forward—changing assembly jobs from line work to bench work, rotation of equally narrow tasks among members of a work group, or increasing the number of functions in a line job—established that the division of labor must have some optimal point, and was not simply built into the technology.

If one looks at job subdivision in the framework of the entire production process, focusing attention more broadly than just upon measures of output per man-hour for specific work functions, it is possible to identify the kinds of costs which depend on the breadth of jobs. The content of jobs affects output and the costliness of labor inputs in a variety of ways.

Putting the problem in traditional micro-economic terms, this section of the essay analyzes the factors lying behind the shapes and location of the unit cost curve in figure 3-2. The traditional approach is labelled "Smith-Taylor." We shall proceed to indicate why this formulation is likely to be incorrect. Throughout the section, many of the cost examples will stem from factors external to the "production job" shown on the axis. Inasmuch as total costs cannot be evaluated except in the framework of an organization, this approach should yield insights about the preferences of that organization on the question of job content.

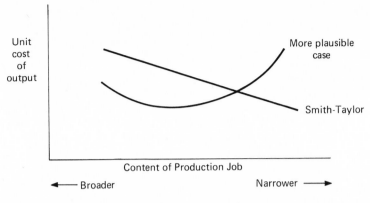

Figure 3-2. Costs and Job Content.

Factors Leading to Cost Declines

Efficiency and Productivity. The rate at which the actual worker can turn out products depends inversely upon the breadth of his job—so wrote Adam Smith. Within some broad limits, this tendency taken alone remains true. There may be a point at which the tedium and goallessness of the work have psychological effects (frustration and conflict) which impede the flow of output. This would seem to certainly be the case if the Taylorian prescription of rigorous separation of all mental work from manual tasks were applied. There are, however, more important factors causing a firm's unit cost curve to turn upwards at some point in the division of labor.

Training Costs. A second factor causing unit costs to fall with increasing specialization is to be found in training times and training costs. In general, the broader the job, the longer is the required period of training. If one considers the case where training takes place within the firm, the following major costs of training a worker to the job can be identified:

1. Costs of supervision—either by taking a trained worker off his job, leading to foregone production, or any losses of output suffered by a general relaxation of supervision elsewhere due to attention given to the learner
2. Foregone production as compared with use of a fully qualified worker. Output is lower for a machine-man combination during the learning process
3. Increased materials wastage, and possible increased wear and tear on the machine.

As the length of the training period—the time elapsed when a new worker performs significantly worse than one with training—is shortened by narrowing the range of duties to be trained, all of these costs are reduced.

Indications of how employer costs vary with breadth of job and training required can be developed from an NICB survey of hiring costs.[19] From figures there given, the following estimates of two important parts of training costs per hire can be derived. It should be emphasized that "salaries of instructors" are only part of the category of supervisory costs mentioned above, while "wage or salary payments of trainees (portion not offset by value of production)" appear to correspond more closely with the foregone production concept.

Insofar as the skilled versus unskilled and semiskilled breakdown accurately reflects differences in job breadth, it can be seen that increasing job specialization does lead to declines in both cost components.

Quality and Availability of the Labor Force. If "fully qualified" workers are abundantly available, then training times in the enterprise become very short—workers reach full productivity almost instantly. In such a case (clearly rather hypothetical) the training cost aspects of choice of job content would vanish. At the other extreme, when workers with even the barest relevant training are not available, the link between labor availability, training times, and job redesign away from breadth becomes stronger. The importance of these factors has been evident in recent years: on the one hand in adjustments to scarcities of skilled workers, and on the other, in attempts to find jobs for unskilled, minority group workers.[20]

Factors Leading to Increases in Unit
Costs as Work is Subdivided

Work Quality and Quality Control. One of the discoveries of the job enlargement school centered upon the relationship between job content and the fraction of work which met standards of quality. When workers were made responsible for a greater number of tasks than usually associated with assembly line jobs, the proportion of work rejected generally fell. There are several reasons for this, although the "psychological" argument—that increased interest content to work

Table 3-1
Training Costs by Skill Level

	Manufacturing		Non-Manufacturing	
	Skilled	Unskilled & Semi-Skilled	Skilled	Unskilled & Semi-Skilled
Instructors' Salaries	$ 8.12	$ 6.60	$ 9.31	$ 8.82
Foregone Production	$205.75	$56.05	$21.64	$13.92.

leads to better motivated, more accurate work—has tended to dominate the literature. Prominent among the other reasons are those based on the amount of supervisory function designed into the job.[21] When one worker is concerned with a large segment of a process, it is clear that responsibility for inferior work can be traced more accurately and swiftly to its source. As jobs are further and further broken down, particularly when the micro-jobs are part of a long assembly line, one loses the ability to exploit the reservoir of self-supervision which each worker possesses. Thus, quality of work should suffer with excessive subdivision.[22]

Supervisory Costs. Closely related to the question of quality control are the unit costs of supervision and management. When jobs are very narrow, supervision becomes external to them. In principle, this would work very well in a plant where procedures and product mix never changed, but this is not the likely case. Exceedingly narrow jobs lead to a need for increased direct supervision where any change is to be made in the status quo. The flexibility in this regard which may come from broader jobs (and the training functions built into them) has in the case of finely divided jobs to be obtained through the use of more widespread supervision.

Work Force Stability. There appears to be evidence that narrower jobs are related to work force characteristics which generate higher unit costs. Absenteeism and levels of labor turnover seem to have been reduced by various experiments in job enlargement.[23] The psychological benefits of broader jobs may account for this in part—increasing psychic income (that catchall explanation), in effect raising the worker's real wage. On the other hand, if broader jobs reflect "humanization of work," the need for recuperation from the tedium and exhaustion which are associated with narrow jobs should be reduced. This would lead to reductions in the amount of down-time required by individual workers and affect the ability of the firm to retain its work force.[24]

Cost Effects Which Are Less Clear

The level of job content chosen by management will have impacts on a wide variety of other variables. The six factors discussed above had fairly clear impacts upon unit costs. There are several other effects which must be mentioned, but for which no general rule can be formulated.

Capital Costs. As jobs are further subdivided, what happens to capital-output ratios or "the period of production?" Experience gives us very little guidance on this question. Consistent with increasing labor productivity as a function of subdivision are a number of impacts upon capital costs. The level of goods-in-process per worker (and hence inventory costs) should be affected by the choice (for example) between bench and line jobs. The period of time required for a unit of product to appear can also be altered by the design of work.

Flexibility. Clearly narrow jobs and narrowly experienced workers reduce the size of internal labor pools which can be drawn upon to fill a job which is temporarily open due to illness or other cause of absence. At the extreme, this could produce inabilities to fill the job in the short run, hence increasing costs.[25] On the other side of the coin, however, it is possible that narrowly specialized jobs may be easier (and less costly) to fill in the long run from the general external labor market.

Industrial Relations and Control of the Work Place. The costs and benefits in this regard are difficult to quantify, but it is clear that the kinds of jobs in an enterprise will affect the operation of its industrial relations system. The various substantive rules on pay methods, job and promotion rights of workers, lay-offs, and so forth, will be affected by the content of the jobs in existence. Moreover, the balance of power between the actors in the system (and hence, management's sense of control over the work place) will be involved. It is clear that, in the good old days, narrow job division made individual workers much more dispensable and replaceable, giving management extensive control of the actions at the work place. Narrow job design can eliminate or weaken those parts of the technology which give rise to strategic jobs from the point of view of unionism and collective bargaining.

A Summary Model of Unit Costs and
Employer Preferences

The factors affecting unit costs discussed above can now be presented in summary form. Such an overall survey will emphasize the fact that the coexistence of these effects poses questions of choice of job content in the light of varying production costs. The problem becomes the choice of an *optimal* bundle of jobs with which to accomplish a certain quantity of work.

At this stage, the formal model must be greatly simplified. At the price of some analytical clarity and brevity, the assumptions involved are unsatisfactory from the point of view of practical life and theoretical generality. However, the model will make clear the operations of job design from the employer's point of view.

In order to be able to reduce the problem to one of minimizing costs for a fixed level of output (i.e., specific amount of work to be performed), consider a department of a firm producing a certain commodity. The work of the department is to get the commodity from one stage of completion to another, or to produce a part of the final commodity. Thus the price and output (Q^o below) of the total commodity can be taken as fixed; the duty of the department manager is to minimize unit costs in this stage of processing.

Another (more realistic) assumption is that the wage rate is fixed by the market *and* is invariate with respect to the nature and content of the job. This assumption is only one of many that could be made, but simplifies matters at this stage.

The factors entering employers' decisions are thus listed, with the probable signs of their derivatives. In the expression below, n is number of workers, b is the breadth of job.[a]

(1) Smith's Law: $\dfrac{Q}{n}$ (average *gross* labor productivity) $= p(b)\, p'(b) \leqslant 0$

(2) Definition: $n = \dfrac{Q^o}{q_n}$, where q_n is *net* output per worker [see (9) below].

(3) Training costs for a worker per unit of time measured as lost production:[b] $C_{t_1} = t_1\,(b)$ $t_1'(b) \geqslant 0$

(4) Training time for a worker: $C_{t_2} = t_2\,(b)$ $t_2'(b) \geqslant 0$

(5) Turnover effect expressed as Expected Time of Worker Retention: $e_W = e\,(b)$ $e'(b) \geqslant 0$

(6) Supervisory costs: $C_S = S(n,b)$ $\dfrac{\partial S}{\partial n} \geqslant 0,\ \dfrac{\partial S}{\partial b} \leqslant 0$

(7) Capital costs per unit of output: $C_k = K(n,b)$ $\dfrac{\partial K}{\partial n} = ?,\ \dfrac{\partial K}{\partial b} = ?$

(8) Wastage and quality control costs per unit of output: $C_w = W(b)$ $W'(b) \leqslant 0$

Hence, from the above set of effects, it appears that the output net of training costs per worker per unit of time can be expressed as:

(9)
$$q_n = \frac{p\,(b)\, e\,(b) - t_1\,(b)\, t_2\,(b)}{e(b)}$$

and we may reformulate (2) above as:

(10)
$$n = \frac{Q^o}{\dfrac{p\,(b)\, e\,(b) - t_1\,(b)\, t_2\,(b)}{e\,(b)}}$$

[a]We leave aside the problem of what such an index of job breadth would look like.
[b]It is recognized that, in reality, such costs will be large at the outset of training and eventually approach zero. Here they are averaged over the training time.

Total costs of production in this department are the sum of capital, supervisory, wastage and labor costs (the latter defined to include training costs):

(11) $C = Q^O K(n,b) + Q^O S(n,b) + W(b) + \bar{w}n$, where $\bar{w}$ is the market wage rate.

Writing the wage bill as $\dfrac{\bar{w}Q^O}{q_n}$, then unit costs can be expressed as

(12) $\bar{c} = K(n,b) + S(n,b) + W(b) + \dfrac{\bar{w}}{q_n}$.

This equation can be differentiated and set equal to zero in the traditional manner. While the results seem economically meaningful and reasonable, it may be more fruitful to look at the problem graphically. After all, if we were to prove that the resulting system of equations is truly a minimum cost solution, we would have to establish that $\dfrac{\partial^2 c}{\partial b^2} > 0$, etc. In light of our uncertainty about the second derivatives of most of the functions above, it will be just as well to go ahead and make the assumptions underlying the well-behaved curves below without spending more time differentiating equations.

Let us redefine some of the functions above, so that all costs are expressed on a per-unit basis, so that the diagrams below can be developed. In Figure 3-3 are shown the expected shapes of the various cost curves associated with a constant output and variations in the breadth of job, taking into account any effects upon the number of workers which stem from changing job content. The *levels* of the curves are of less importance than their shapes.

Thus in figure 3-3 we see the following:

1. Although the wage rate $(\bar{w})$ is independent of breadth of job and the number

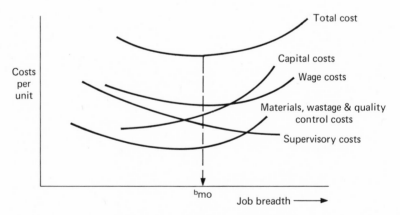

Figure 3-3. Costs and Job Breadth.

of workers, unit wage costs change as productivity and training costs are affected. This is shown separately in figure 3-4 below.

2. Supervisory costs fall as the supervisory function is incorporated with production work by job enlargement.
3. Materials, wastage and quality control costs are high for broad jobs (as Adam Smith would have it), declining with increased specialization, but are also high in very narrow jobs, as workers become less motivated and/or penalized for their errors.
4. Capital costs per worker rise on the assumption that capital/labor ratios fall more slowly than the length of the period of production rises: direct capital cost decreases (if any) are more than offset by increases in inventory cost of goods in process.

Given the arguments (1) through (4), it is likely that the per-unit total cost curve will look roughly like that shown.

The shape of q_n above is based upon the following assumptions:

1. Training costs and training times cannot fall without limit as the job becomes narrower.
2. Given a fixed Q^o, $p'(b)$ (rate of change of average labor productivity) is positive for very narrow job breadths.
3. Turnover effects (reducing the average stay on the job and thereby increasing per unit training costs over the lifetime of the man-job relationship) are important.

If the above assumptions about q_n and the various components of costs are correct, then the unit cost curve will have the shape indicated in figure 3-3: b_{mo}

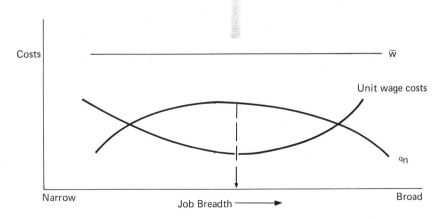

Figure 3-4. Derivation of Unit Wage Costs.

will be the optimal job content from the point of view of management.

A further possibility should be mentioned. It may be that changes in the content of jobs are associated with an employer's ability to recruit his workers from a different class of labor. Graphically, this would mean that the wage line in figure 3-4 would be positively sloped. As work became further and further subdivided, firms could hire those with lower skills and less education, possibly from social or ethnic groups which were "exploitable."

Worker Preferences and Job Breadth

Observed phenomena in the workplace strongly suggest that workers have an interest in the breadth of content of their jobs. Probably the clearest and quickest example which comes to mind concerns the traditional crafts in the construction industry. In these crafts, apprentices put in a good deal of time, at a cost in foregone earnings, in learning a fairly broad range of functions involving differing materials and products. Moreover, the unions in this industry devote a great deal of time and energy to defending the range of work which falls within the contractual and technical competence of their members. Nor are these groups immune to the temptation of aggrandizement at the expense of other groups, particularly when new products and processes are being introduced.

As was the case from management's point of view, varying the content of jobs affects the well-being of workers in a number of ways, some detrimental, others beneficial. The result of these impacts is reflected in the "web of rules" that grow up in different plant and industry-wide systems of industrial relations.

In the sections below we shall consider several kinds of forces which stem from the division of labor as they bear upon the welfare of workers. At the end of the section, a formal model is developed to draw all these factors together.

Effects of Job Specialization on
Workers

The Role of Productivity. The increases in output per worker which tend to accompany advancing job specialization play a dual function in affecting worker conditions. The first consideration involves its impact upon the level of employment; the second concerns the relationship between productivity and wages.

In the first case, we are encountering another facet of that set of arguments loosely called the "lump of labor" fallacy. Much as one argues the other side of the coin when considering wage increases, the effect of productivity increase which labor spokesmen most frequently stress is that which bears on the level of employment. Although the dynamic properties of the economy as a whole have led to satisfactory long-run adjustments to increasing productivity, it is equally clear that labor's concern is not always nor uniformly misplaced. In some industries—notably those with stagnant or declining product demand, where the alterations of work techniques will lead to large improvements in productivity—the short-run implications for workers and their organizations have been serious. One can, for example, speculate about the results in the bricklaying trade had Taylor's prescriptions been scrupulously applied[26]—he thought that the productivity gains would be immense. And this would only have been through the reorganization of a largely constant "tools" technology. What are the challenges by comparison when there is a shift in the technology employed, as when prefabricated materials are introduced to supplant the ancient trade?

Workers and their organizations are thus concerned, as we can see from the last example, not only with direct redesign of the job that they hold currently, but with the development of products and processes which serve as an alternative to their way of getting a certain output created. In such cases, workers and their organizations often attempt to prohibit use of materials produced in ways which reduce their work, or at least to control the work which remains and incorporate the new methods or products into their jurisdiction. The case of Chicago stonecutters circa 1890, well described by George E. Barnett, is an interesting example of this process. In reaction to the mechanization of stone finishing by the stoneplaner, the unions followed a variety of policies—prohibition of the machine, exclusion of plane-cut stone from local markets, enforced employment of craftsmen in the machine-centered jobs which in fact required lesser skills—all of which are clearly aimed at maintaining employment levels for the craftsmen involved.[27]

The job content-productivity relationship and its employment effects have been stressed far more than the connection between productivity and wage levels. In part this can be explained by a tendency for concern to be placed upon short-run problems whereas the long run—in which the wage effect presumably appears—can take care of itself. Moreover, the relationship between the breadth of jobs and wage levels is fairly complicated.

In the long run, almost any theory of wages (except cost-of-production-of-labor versions) would lead one to expect increased productivity to be reflected in the wage rates of labor services. Thus, if productivity per man is increased by division of labor, wages should be higher for it. Historically, this effect is intertwined with the rise in capital-labor ratios which accompany advancing mechanization, so that the finer division of labor which often accompanies mechanization may be overlooked. It does, however, provide a good Smithian explanation for the size-of-establishment wage differentials described by Lester.[28]

Insofar as narrowing the content of a given job reduces the amount of training costs which a worker bears, the problem becomes further confused. After all, most conventional wage theory and all wage measurements include the return on human capital as part of the wage. If (as seems the likely case), the return on human capital investments far exceeds that on any alternative investment which a worker is able to make, then workers may wish to retain this investment option as a means of gaining higher income. In such a case, the equally long-run impact of job narrowing on wages may be offset by reductions in the human capital source of worker earnings. There are difficulties in the interpretation of rates of return on human capital (embodied in blue-collar skills) as truly independent variables which enter into worker choices, although they should be noted for completeness. For the time being, if we do follow the common treatment as found in the literature on human capital, we may assume that the incorporation of investment opportunities in the content of jobs has conceptual significance. It will become obvious, though, that in practice its importance should be swamped by other considerations.

Effects on Work Probability. As suggested above, any productivity advances which reduce the total number of man-hours required have an effect on the overall probability of finding work. The importance of job and training breadth is central to our understanding of worker policies to affect employment probabilities.[29]

These policies fall into four broad categories, usually found in reality in one form or another of symbiosis. The ways of trying to moderate changes in (or increase the actual levels of) employment probabilities operate through effects on product and labor markets, the interpersonal and intertemporal allocation of work, and the adaptability of workers to a range of job options.

First, the product market (and hence level of demand for workers) can be affected in a variety of ways. Examples include promotional campaigns (advertising of products by labor organizations, union labels, and so forth).

Second, the tightness of particular labor markets can be controlled to some extent by exclusionary policies, which have a similar impact upon probabilities of finding employment. These two types of policies are indirectly related to the breadth of job content and training which workers' organizations will seek, as—to be effective—the workers or their organizations must be able to deliver the requisite skills and workers necessary to perform the work involved.

Thirdly, the probabilities of employment can also be affected through manipulating the distribution of work through time in attempts to smooth out fluctuations. The nineteenth-century attempts by coal miners in the United States to prevent the operators from accumulating sizable inventories improved their bargaining power but also would assure a higher level of employment during periods of depression. Again, policies of spreading the work across the labor force (as is the case in the printing trades when work is scarce) will tend to produce a more equitable distribution of employment opportunities among members. Such policies are indirectly related to the nature of jobs and the training of workers, since extreme specialization of tasks and the corresponding worker skills would hinder the implementation of such redistributive policies.

Finally, although it is closely interwoven with the policies listed above, it is important to stress the value of broad job content and broadly trained workers in smoothing out the inevitable fluctuations in employment probabilities. The broader the work to be performed which is controlled by a group of workers (or their organization) and the broader their training and job, the better situated they are when confronted by economic and technological changes. Cyclical fluctuations in employment in narrow markets (narrow in product-line or geographical dimensions) can be escaped to some extent by transfer of labor to other regions or products. When an automobile assembly line or meat-packing plant shuts down, the unemployment impact upon the line workers is distinctly different than the effects upon the maintenance craftsmen. The line skills are few and not easily transferred; the craftsmen are more broadly trained, encompass more functions within their job, and can move to other employment.

Much the same holds true with adaptability to technological change. On the one hand, broadly trained workers in broad jobs can be adapted to new functions, or (as with the glass bottle blowers) they control the earlier process so thoroughly that they are able to control the introduction of new technology and assure that—even if the new technology cannot be defeated—the work which remains falls into their hands.

The investment in apprenticeship training is one of the principal methods whereby this flexibility is achieved. Critics of apprenticeship programs should recognize that these programs, which have served to control the supply of labor in a trade (and to impose social costs by excluding certain groups, notably blacks), are not only based on rational preferences of workers, but that the social benefits are not negligible. Broadly skilled workers with a wide range of job adaptability are more likely to find new work and less likely to impose welfare and retraining costs upon the community.[30]

Effects Upon Training Costs Borne by Workers. That the breadth and content of jobs are directly related to the training times entailed should seem clear. There is therefore an element of cost involved in choosing broader jobs and longer training times. Perhaps a more interesting question can be posed: how does the varying content of the job affect the proportions in which this cost is borne by workers and employers? More generally, is there something else operating with or behind Becker's "general-specific" distinction which depends on job content? The latter problem will be investigated below; for the time being let us simply assume that worker-borne costs rise with broadening jobs. It is difficult to say prima facie whether this is consistent with Becker's conclusions or not.

From the worker's point of view, considering either a typical apprenticeship program or employment under an incentive system, the training costs are the amount by which his wage falls short of alternatives available during the training period plus any actual out-of-pocket costs involved. For an example of the magnitude of the foregone earnings component, as well as some of the methodological difficulties in measuring it, let us consider the case of apprentices. This case is doubly appropriate in view of the occasional doubts in some quarters whether apprentices actually do suffer losses from foregone earnings during training. The evidence suggests that they do, and that the amounts are not small.

Jacob Mincer estimated the foregone earnings of apprentices in three crafts as falling in a range from $400 to $1,000 per year of training based upon 1950 census income data.[31] The size of the cost estimates depended to a large degree upon the measure chosen for an alternative wage rate. Mincer employed three different yardsticks for this purpose: (a) all operatives in the same industry; (b) operatives with educational attainment levels equal to those of apprentices (which are greater than the all-operative average); and (c) all operatives in the industry, adjusted for an assumed return of 10 percent on the additional formal education of apprentices. The reader should consult Mincer's article for details, as well as general theoretical treatment of the question of on-the-job training.

Somewhat similar figures, which avoid the dubious comparison with "operatives" have been derived by the author from union agreements for Eastern Massachusetts construction trades. In keeping with national standards,[32] the local agreements specify apprentice rates as fractions of the journeyman wage at various points in the apprenticeship period.

The standard taken for foregone earnings is the laborer's wage—which for the Boston area was $3.60 per hour and $.30 fringe. This is a good measure insofar as it reflects natural proclivities and talent that might impel one towards a construction job; and may include monopoly gains which a comparison with average hourly earnings in manufacturing would not. It is a bad measure (that is, overstates foregone earnings) to the extent that apprenticeship employment is more regular than laborer employment; if the converse is true, it will understate the costs involved.

Let us consider the apprentice pay scales for the two crafts shown in Table 3-2.

Table 3-2
Foregone Earnings of Apprentices: Boston, 1967

| Cement Masons | | Carpenters | |
(Journeyman rate $5.05 + 35¢ contribution to pension, health and welfare fund)		(Journeyman rate $5.55 + 40¢ PHW)	
1st 3 months	50%	1st 6 months	50%
Next 3 months	55	2nd 6 months	55
Next 12 months	65	3rd 6 months	60
Next 6 months	70	4th 6 months	65
Next 6 months	75	5th 6 months	70
Next 6 months	85	6th 6 months	75
		7th 6 months	80
		8th 6 months	85

Arranging the data by six month periods, we find the following "foregone earnings" (−) or "increased earnings" (+) as compared with the laborers' rate:[33]

Table 3-2 (cont.)

	Cement Masons	Carpenters
1st 6 months	$−1294.80	$−1164.80
2nd 6 months	− 644.80	− 884.00
3rd 6 months	− 644.80	− 644.80
4th 6 months	− 374.40	− 301.60
5th 6 months	− 114.40	− 20.80
6th 6 months	+ 405.60	+ 270.40
7th 6 months	Program Completed	+ 561.60
8th 6 months		+ 852.82
Net	−2667.60	−1331.20

Interestingly, the foregone earnings over the two and a half year period before one reaches the laborer rate are almost identical in the carpentry program (3016.00) and the program for cement masons (3073.20).

A number of minor economic factors which could bear upon the optimal choice of job content from the worker's vantage point have been neglected at this stage. Among them are the relationships among job content, wage costs, prices and product demand, and the amount of transfer costs associated with moving from one employer (or assignment) to another in a broad content job. Also left aside have been any connections between job breadth and product quality which might have an independent effect upon price and demand levels for the finished product.

These dynamic relationships which exist among costs, wages, technology, output and overall levels of unemployment are as demanding of investigation as the static, myopic analysis of factors leading to a "job control" mentality. Examples are not hard to find—given a sufficient strength of worker organizations it might have been possible for the buggy and bicycle makers whose jobs were threatened by the automobile to have maintained handicraft methods and strong job control for their members. This would have had the short-run effects on employment probability that we have sketched, but would gross employment in the industry have risen so rapidly and to such levels if the costs of production had been as high as craft methods would dictate? The answer is clear, even though employment probabilities for the individual worker may have been rendered more variable at all points in time. Seniority systems reflect one approach to ameliorating employment probabilities for workers in narrowly defined jobs closely tied to one industry. Their employment probabilities go up as their potential for retraining and mobility declines.

Psychic Costs of Narrow Jobs. Psychological and sociological investigators have long dwelt upon the dissatisfactions that come from finely divided jobs. A variety of impacts upon employers' costs have been mentioned above—turnover, absenteeism, responsibility—which would stem from workers' frustrations, irritations, and general low morale. It must further be supposed that the tedium, lack of responsibility or independence, and absence of clear purpose to the work associated with extreme division of labor impose psychic costs upon individual workers. The literature on these questions is immense—the writings of Georges Friedman (*Industrial Society: The Anatomy of Work*), Adam Abruzzi (*Work, Workers and Work Measurement*), and Daniel Bell (*Work and its Discontents*) are well known.[34] In determining workers' preferences, we therefore postulate the existence of a level of psychic costs directly related to degree of specialization.[35]

A Static Model of Worker Preferences

Returning to the simple framework developed earlier in "A Summary Model of Unit Costs and Employer Preferences," let us draw together the influences upon worker choice of job breadth in a basic "job control" model. There follows a listing of the principal functional relationships discussed above, with indications of the probable signs of some of their derivatives.

(1) Productivity-wage nexus $w = f(b)$ $f'(b) < 0$ (at least for some range of b)

(2) Employment probabilities for a "closed group" $P_e = g(b)$ $g'(b) > 0$

(3) Expected earnings of a worker $E(Y) = w \cdot P_e = f(b)g(b)$

(4) Training costs borne by workers

$$T_w = \sum_{t=1}^{t_t(b)} t_w(b)\, t_t(b)$$

where $t_w(b)$ is the cost per time period and $t_t(b)$ is the length of that period, both as functions of b, the breadth of jobs.

(5) The "disutility of labor" as affected by tedium, worker irritation and loss of psychic income is also a function of job specialization, and is lumped together as psychic costs.

$$\Psi = \Psi(b) \qquad\qquad \Psi(b)' < 0$$

In such a case, workers' maximand will be as shown below, with T_w being workers' time-horizon length and r, their rate of time preference.

(6) Max $\displaystyle \sum_{t=1}^{T_w} \frac{P_e \cdot w}{(1+r)_t} - \sum_{t=1}^{t_t(b)} \frac{t_w(b)\, t_t(b)}{(1+r)_t} - \sum_{t=1}^{T_w} \frac{\Psi(b)}{(1+r)_t}$

which will be maximized when

$$(7) \quad \sum_{t=1}^{T_w} \frac{P_e' w + P_e w'}{(1+r)^t} - \sum_{t=1}^{t_t(b)} \frac{t'_w(b) t_t(b) + t_w(b) t_{t'}(b)}{(1+r)^t} - \sum_{t=1}^{T_w} \frac{\Psi'(b)}{(1+r)^t} = 0.$$

Having produced a formal result that looks both meaningful economically and solvable as a function of only one variable, b, let us then retreat to a graphical analysis comparable to that given for management. The principal influences on economic benefits are shown in figure 3-5.

From figure 3-5, a curve of net economic benefits can be obtained (by subtraction of the training-cost curve from the probable discounted earnings curve) which should have the shape shown in figure 3-6. In the latter diagram, the benefits are compared with the psychic costs to show the optimal division of labor from the worker's point of view, b_{wo}.

Some Evidence Supporting the Model

The model of worker preferences utilized in this chapter cannot be tested in its entirety, but one of the most important behavioral assumptions fortunately can be subjected to statistical scrutiny. The hypothesis that worker choices on job and training breadth are dependent upon expected earnings implies that those

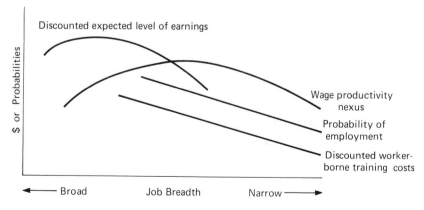

Figure 3-5. Job Breadth and Workers' Costs and Benefits.

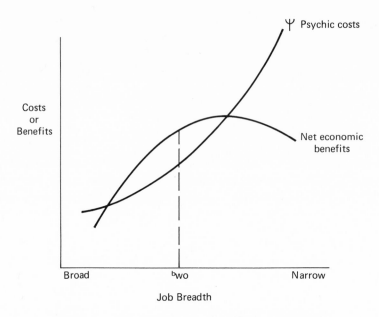

Figure 3-6. Psychic Costs and Net Economic Benefits.

whose income expectations are low will feel a greater need for broader training than those workers with higher employment probabilities and wage rate expectations. The existence of this latter relationship can be tested with the results of a 1956 sample of former apprentices.

Between January and June 1956 the Bureau of Apprenticeship and Training, U.S. Department of Labor, surveyed 3,278 persons who had completed training programs in 1950.[36] The sample covered roughly 8.5% of the individuals completing apprenticeship in that year. The coverage of the survey is fortunate for the purpose of testing our hypothesis, as a number of factors—educational levels, family backgrounds, interest in the "manual arts"—are likely to be more homogeneous for this group than for the labor force as a whole.[37] Moreover, there is reason to think that the opinions expressed—particularly for the building trades—are likely to be based upon individuals' direct observations of their employment success in comparison with other journeymen.

In tables 2, 3, and 4 of the *BAT Bulletin*, the former apprentices reported their employment status (employed, unemployed, sick or out of the labor force), current position (journeyman, supervisor, employer, and so on), and their average hourly wage rate, respectively. The employment rate corresponds to the employment probabilities in the theory, while the percentage of former apprentices who have advanced to foreman or employer status is an index of promotion possibilities and their demands upon the worker's skills. The wage rate is a "weak" variable, as it does not pertain to journeymen alone, but includes some influences of promotion and advancement.

With regard to the dependent variable—preference on job and training breadth—the former apprentices were asked how their training on the job could have been improved. For the group as a whole, 23.5% of the suggestions for improvement were concerned with broader training. Variations in this response among the several trade groups should, under our hypothesis, be directly related to the unemployment rate (UE), and promotion rates (P, the proportion of former apprentices who reported status of supervisor, foreman, employer or contractor), and inversely related to the level of wage rates. A simple unweighted least-squares regression of the percentage wanting broader training (B) against the three variables influencing expected income gives the following result, with t values in parentheses. The relationship is easily significant at the 1% level.

$$B = 40.9 + 6.6 \ UE + .4P - 11.6w$$
$$\quad (1.3) \quad (6.5) \quad\quad (7.5) \quad (1.5) \quad\quad\quad R^2 = .98$$

A similar substantiation of the behavioral hypothesis concerning job and training preferences of workers is suggested by the results of a Labor Department study of MDTA program completers as reported by Mangum. To quote his summary: "The completers (as compared with drop-outs) were somewhat more likely to be nonwhite and *to have had longer unemployment and less successful labor market experience* before entering training."[38] Thus, in the case of workers who are far less favorably situated to be aware of training payoffs from personal or family experience, and who are often alleged to have higher rates of time preference than craftsmen, some supporting evidence appears.

The Determination of Job and Training Breadth

In order to make clear the relationships and ideas proposed, the discussion above has been stated in terms of job breadth alone. Obviously, this is only part of the story—workers and managers are equally concerned with the breadth of training which goes along (but is not identical) with the breadth of the job. Thus, when we try to bring together the preferences of workers and managers in a single model, it is necessary to introduce training breadth as an explicit variable.

As far as workers are concerned, broader training has many of the same characteristics of broader jobs. Given a certain job breadth (which is associated with the same level of required training), we may analyze the costs and benefits to workers and managers from additional training beyond that strictly necessary.

When a worker absorbs training beyond the demands of his immediate job, he is likely to accrue a number of additional benefits. The benefits are in part dependent upon the nature of the "excess training" which he builds up. If the training is closely related to his current job, then he improves his employment probabilities as far as the particular shop or industry is concerned. An example would be the narrowly trained operator of a machine tool who learns to operate a different piece of equipment. This sort of training has two general benefits upon his future employment expectations—to increase the chances of working through greater lateral mobility and to train him for possible promotion to a supervisory or "utility" position. It is important to remember that, in this regard, the breadth of the job interlocks with the breadth of training to keep the range of skills "sharp"—reinforcing the effects of broader training.

Training which is not closely related to the skill demands of the man's current job may also affect his future employment probabilities in other occupations or industries. In this regard, the recent case of an MBTA trolley driver who earned an A.B. at Harvard through ten years of extension study would be a clear example. There would be perhaps very few situations in which a man's excess training was less related to his performance and employment expectations in his current job. While the greater part of the trolley driver's accumulation of knowledge may reflect personal consumption, it cannot be denied that almost any training experience is at least moderately related to future employment possibilities.

Whether or not "excess training" is closely allied to the nature of the man's current job, many of the arguments made about impacts on employment probabilities hold equally for the future course of his wages. Additional knowledge and skills can make a man more productive at his tasks, perhaps increase his earnings directly. Alternatively, there will be effects on wages through promotions which are more likely to go to the better trained, more knowledgeable and skilled employees.

The importance of promotability in the craft as well as beyond it (by moving to employer status) can be suggested by the figures in table 3-3. They refer to the percentage of apprentices by craft who had advanced to supervisory positions or employer status six years after completion of their apprenticeship.

The two separate effects on probable frequency of employment and probable

Table 3-3
Advancement in Status Six Years After Apprenticeship

Crafts	% Supervisors or Foremen	% Contractors or Employers
Building Trades	19.7	9.6
Metal Trades	15.3	1.0
Mechanic and Repair Trades	18.5	7.1
Printing Trades	16.7	1.1
Other	18.9	12.5
All	18.7	8.0

Source: Bureau of Apprenticeship and Training, "Career Patterns of former Apprentices," Bulletin T-147, March 1959, table 3.

wage levels combine to yield benefits through raising the level of the individual's stream of expected earnings. Against these benefits (appropriately discounted) must be set any additional expenditures which the worker incurs as the cost of broader training. Training beyond the need of the current job involves a variety of costs in the form of direct expenditures and foregone earnings.

As a matter of pure speculation, it should be mentioned that training beyond the needs of the job may affect the psychic costs borne by the worker in a number of ways. Knowledge of the world that lies beyond the confines of the daily set of tasks may increase dissatisfaction or decrease it. The case studies which touch on this subject are inconclusive, to say the least; and they have generally focused sharply on the worker's feelings of contentment. Probably a good deal depends upon the pace and rhythm of the daily job. Jobs in which spaces of vacant time arise—such as the Boston carman's case noted above—allow learning beyond the job to be dovetailed with existing inadequacies of the current job and lead to reduced costs of broadened training as well as immediate direct satisfaction. A number of case studies would indicate that in less unusual circumstances, broader training—for example, learning the job of the other operators in a small work group—has beneficial effects upon worker morale and satisfaction.

Managements also have a substantial concern with the training breadth of their workers, above and beyond the demands of the job itself. In the first place, training broader than strictly required has often been a part of the screening process for new employment applicants. Beyond the simple notion that more broadly trained workers, if available, are likely to be more productive and less costly to employ, there exists the desire to hire individuals with some part of the broader skills needed for jobs above the entry level. The much-bewailed high school diploma requirements for sweeper and low-grade clerical jobs were partially founded on these considerations. Moreover, in the recursive world of job and skill ladders, OJT and promotion, such selection procedures make economic sense.

Abstracting from such dynamic considerations, the breadth of worker training is a matter of interest even in a static case with a given job breadth for the individual. More broadly trained workers allow management greater flexibility in the scheduling of work and workers. Workers with training above the strict minimum are more adaptable to changes in equipment used and product mixes. Moreover, there are likely to be some economies in supervision through the employment of better trained workers.

Possibly the greatest economies from a flexible work force would stem from the reduction of hiring and layoff costs.[39] If a plant employs very narrowly trained workers, small changes in the mix of product demand or equipment characteristics would necessitate layoff of one outmoded worker and hiring of another to replace him, or the institution of a program to retrain the worker. Both hiring and laying off workers cost money; and crash retraining programs are likely to be relatively expensive. As many of the wage costs of modern firms are no longer "variable" in the true sense of the word, emphasis on worker adaptability is likely to be increased in the foreseeable future.

Against the benefits which the firm derives from employing workers trained beyond the needs of their day-to-day jobs must be set any additional costs imposed upon the firm. For the most part, these extra expenses would depend upon the share of costs of broader training which the firm must bear.[40] These costs would stem from the same considerations of lost production, redirection of supervisory resources, materials wastage, and formal training course expenses outlined earlier.

We may summarize much of the foregoing in graphical form, beginning with figure 3-7 below, which shows the relationships between breadth of job and breadth of training from the employer's point of view. Job breadth, it must be recalled, is viewed as defining the narrowest possible equilibrium level of training which will suffice.

Thus, the dotted 45° line shows all those minimal job training pairs; no combinations below that line are feasible. Moreover, the hard facts of the underlying technology impose a limited range upon the variations possible in job breadth compatible with performing a certain quantity of work. These possibilities are indicated by the solid line TT, within which range choices must be made.

From the arguments in foregoing sections, it would seem that employers' iso-cost curves can be drawn: $c_o, \ldots c_i \ldots c_n$ as shown in figure 3-6. These lines tell us that unit costs of production remain the same for varying combinations of job breadth and training. They are given their particular shape to incorporate the expected returns to training outlined earlier. Given a certain job breadth, as employees become more broadly trained the firm takes advantage of any econo-

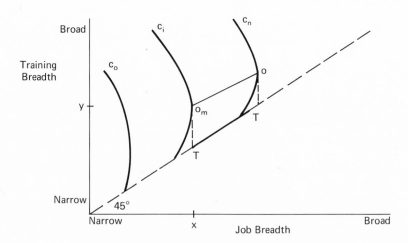

Figure 3-7. Employers' Iso-Cost Curves.

mies of supervision and advantages of flexibility and moves to lower unit cost curves. At some point, however, training costs borne by the company and possible losses of company-wide productivity stemming from the large amounts of OJT being accomplished should cause the iso-cost curves to bend backward as shown, so that increasing training leads to higher production costs. As should be obvious, the arguments about the particular shape of the curves are less important than the conceptual apparatus involved.

In order to put out the fixed level of work underlying the iso-cost curves, the firm would choose the minimum cost feasible solution, namely the point on iso-cost curve c_i labelled O_M corresponding in this case to the minimum job breadth x and a training breadth of y. The line $O_M O$ shows the set of similar combinations reflecting the "second-best" optima for other, broader jobs.

Workers' preferences can be analyzed in the same fashion, as shown in figure 3-8. Given the same technologically-fixed range of possible job breadths, we can draw a series of iso-benefit curves, $b_0, \ldots b_i, \ldots b_n$. These iso-benefit curves reflect all the considerations of both worker benefits and costs discussed above. They are drawn on the assumption that, for a given job breadth, workers move to higher levels of net economic and psychological benefit through the accumulation of additional training. At some point, however, the advantages of improved employment probabilities are more than offset by increases in training costs (both direct costs and foregone earnings) borne by the worker. We note in passing that the position and shape of these curves (as well as those for managers) can be manipulated through shifting the costs of training between the parties or to a third party such as the state.

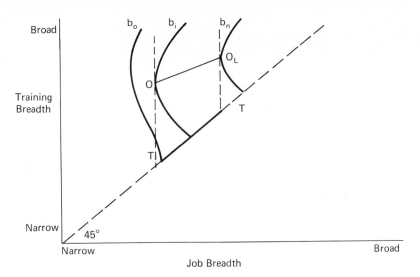

Figure 3-8. Workers' Iso-Benefit Curves.

In figure 3-8, we can easily see that within the limits imposed by technology, the very best that a worker could do would be to attain point O_L. The worker's reaction curve, if forced to accept a narrower job, would be described by the line $O_L O$.

Several subsidiary points should be raised before launching into a discussion of the process whereby workers and managers may reach agreement on job and training breadth.

1. Is it not possible, for a variety of reasons, that managers' cost or workers' benefit curves are not arrayed with the pleasing monotonic increasing or decreasing levels hypothesized? For time-paid jobs, with a fixed wage rate, such a possibility seems remote indeed, but matters may be different for piece work jobs with a set piece rate. In such a case, worker productivity may be sufficiently increased by specialization that a reversal of the above ordering might come about. Such a possibility is, however, fully comparable with the analytical framework developed—in a case of this sort, workers' and managers' preferences would run in the same direction.

2. Given the possible scope for job breadth TT, in what relationship do the managers' and workers' optima stand? Tersely put: is $O_L O'$ likely to be generally above or below $O_M O$? Judging from general observations of the world, it would seem that for most blue-collar jobs in tight labor markets, workers' preferences will involve a broader level of training than optimal from management's point of view. Basically this is a restatement of an impression that broadening the worker's training increases managers' flexibility in use of the work force less than it increases potential employment and earnings for workers.

3. The positions and shapes of the curves in figures 3-7 and 3-8 are clearly dependent upon the state of the labor market. Thus, in a loose market with plenty of well-trained workers available, managers' preference curves will be almost perfectly elastic with respect to training—training costs will be very low and hiring costs may be reduced through the expedient rule of thumb of hiring only the "best qualified."

4. The role of workers' organizations in structuring and controlling the workers' preferences may be significant. Labor organizations have a long-run view of training benefits (or at least claim to have this perspective), and can manipulate employment probabilities directly through restrictions upon entry to the craft, semidirectly via the attrition associated with increasing length of training, and by controlling the access of other workers to the work involved. Jurisdictional control by craft unions springs to mind, but the interests of industrial unions in job design, redesign and elimination are analogous, although the primary focus shifts to wage rates and immediate questions of worker redundancy.[41] Moreover, the role of workers' organizations in altering the Beckerian meaning of "general" and "specific" must be noted. Training which is of general applicability in an industry but specific to that industry alone may, via industry-wide unionization, affect the individual employer in the same way as training specific to his firm.

5. The assumption of constancy of wages regardless of current job breadth is obviously unrealistic. Within the model as described in figures 3-7 and 3-8, with a narrow and continuous range of choices (TT), the assumption is not unbearably restrictive. However, it is more likely in fact that choices will be much more disparate, and furthermore discontinuous, with major jumps from one set of alternatives to another. When facing these choices, it is likely that employers will confront changes in the wage rate depending on the class of workers involved. Thus, by decomposing garment trades jobs (so that current practice is to subcontract most operations below the cutting stage) it becomes possible to hire workers from a different population (such as blacks), which commands a different wage rate. This much is clear. On the other hand, changing the wage rate by moving to another sector of the labor force does not necessarily have the same impact on production costs. The quality of workers may be much worse, so that the reversal of iso-cost surfaces suggested above may occur.

6. Technological change and the predicted "degradation of labor" (F.A. Walker's phrase) can be understood in this light. The common view has been that mechanization, automation, and the like, lead to technological options lower down on the job and training breadth scales, which can be filled by a different, lower-paid class of workers. The standards and wage scales of these workers will then pull down the standards and status of those "craftsmen" formerly employed. That this process is not inevitable nor obvious should be evident, although the iso-cost curves we have drawn are consistent with continuous employer pressure in that direction.

7. Some of the mechanics underlying the structure of "internal labor markets" and the location of hiring points can be briefly indicated, along with some of the background linkages on choice of job and training breadths. As Doeringer has observed, technology and product mix determine the job structure of a plant, within the degrees of latitude allowed by job design.[42] The purpose of this section, in part, is to add rigor to the discussion of those relationships and flexibilities.

The technology and its flexibility can be depicted in schematic fashion in figure 3-9. To produce a certain amount of product requires with the current state of technology, three grades of workers: A, B, and C. The degree of flexibility which exists in the design of these jobs depends not only upon the width of the intervals A, B, and C, but also upon the degree to which the labor input coefficients a, b, and c can be altered.

The chosen job breadths for A, B, and C classifications will clearly be interdependent, and will furthermore be linked with the input coefficients a, b, c. Thus, broadly jobbed and trained C workers (operatives, say) may not require B workers who can perform broadest possible jobs involving extensive supervision and repair functions, for example. In fact, the choice of a broad C classification may have a direct impact upon the need for B workers, affecting the relative size of their input coefficient, b.[43]

The attainment of minimum cost of production for the firm will be a func-

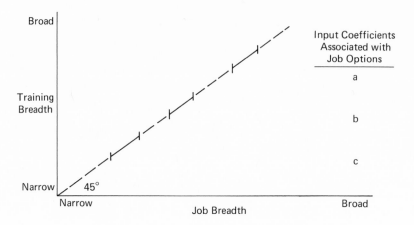

Figure 3-9. Technology and Job Options.

tion of the possible tradeoff between job classes and the wages and other conditions of availability of workers. Thus, if grade A workers have high relative wages
and are hard to come by (physicians), it will be more economical to shift the
production process to heavier reliance on grade B (technicians and the like).

The relationship between the job options for particular grades (graphically
shown as the distance between line segments A, B, and C) is reflected in the
movement patterns of internal labor markets and the location of ports of entry.
Whether workers do or can move up from one grade to another depends upon
(a) the increased training required at the higher classification, and *(b)* the optimal amounts of "excess training" at the lower grade. Figure 3-10 sketches out
this set of considerations, as seen, for simplicity's sake, from management's cost-
oriented viewpoint alone. Classification A is very highly skilled relative to the
others: its minimal performance requirement (t_A) is far in excess of the optimal
training for class B jobs. An optimally trained B worker will not, therefore,
follow a logical path of promotion to grade A: A jobs will be entry points in this
situation. Conversely, an optimal breadth of job and training for grade C workers
will qualify them to perform at least the minimum expected for a B worker. If it
is less expensive to get the C worker to accumulate Δ^t more of training than to
hire an outside worker, B jobs will not ordinarily be ports of entry. C jobs, lying
at the bottom of the ladder, will be a port of entry and a source of supply to
grade B.

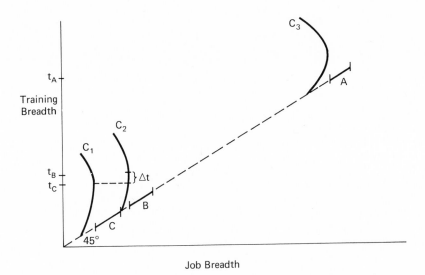

Figure 3-10. Optimal Excess Training.

The Determination of Job and
Training Breadth

It is now time to bring together the preferences of workers and managers which have been sketched out in the preceding pages. In figure 3-11, a set of "well-behaved" iso-cost and iso-benefit curves are shown for a single job of possible breadth range TT. The dependence of both sets of curves upon the costs and benefits of the jobs above and below this one is recalled, and the distances along the 45° line which separates those jobs from the segment TT are assumed to be incorporated in the iso-cost and iso-benefit curves shown.

Under the conditions shown, management would minimize costs at the point Ω_M–choosing a narrow job breadth j_1 and a narrow level of training t_1 of which ET_M reflects the desired amount of "excess training." Workers, on the other hand, would prefer to arrive at the point Ω_L on their highest possible net benefit curve. They seek in this case a broad job (j_2) with broad training (t_2), of which ET_W is training beyond the needs of the jobs itself. The locus of alternative points which are the best that can be done by workers and managers at non-optimal job breadths are shown by R_W and R_M respectively.

The situation which is shown in figure 3-11 roughly corresponds to Gary Becker's category of general training, although it here includes training which is general within the plant as well as between plants. The benefits to workers are high relative to those for management. A situation in which R_M lay above R_W would correspond to "specific training" where the benefits to workers from

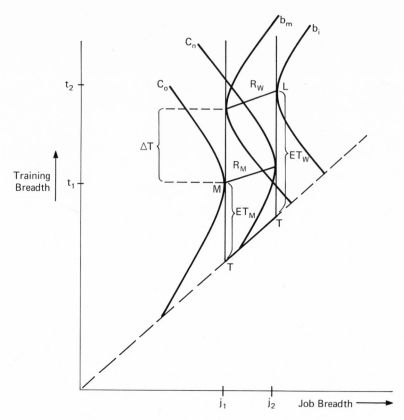

Figure 3-11. Iso-Cost and Iso-Benefit Curves.

additional training are relatively low in comparison with those accruing to management.

Figure 3-11 depicts a disequilibrium situation regarding job and training breadth. Utilizing this fact, we may assess the distribution of training costs as a first step in resolving the disequilibrium. If job breadth j_1 were to be selected—possibly by employer dominance in the labor market—then employers, to reach minimal cost, would be willing to pay for ET_M of "general" training. Thus, factors which influence costs—work force flexibility, labor turnover rates, and so on—have no longer the appearance of a *deus ex machina* (Becker's phrase) but are rather an integral part of the determination not only of job and training breadths, but of the apportionment of their training costs as well. If j_1 is fixed, workers would wish to invest an additional amount ΔT in broader training. In the case of "specific" training where R_M lies above R_W, employers would be willing to assume the entire cost of training. Thus, in this situation, our conclusion agrees with that of Becker, while for general training under our definition, we have come a bit closer to identifying the share of the cost that employers will be willing to pay.

The final link in the chain is closed in the following way—agreement is reached between workers and managers on equilibrium breadth of jobs and training through redistribution of training costs between the parties. The curves in figure 3-11 are based upon one particular distribution of these costs—a shift of costs from managers to workers would move the c_i curves upward, and the b_i curves downward—both toward a point of agreement.

More generally, for any distribution of training costs, there will be a minimum cost job/training-breadth pair for managers, and a corresponding maximum benefit pair for workers. This can be represented by the curve in figure 3-12. For managers, the larger the share of training costs absorbed, the higher will be average costs borne by management. For workers, bearing a greater share of these costs will reduce net benefits for any job/training-breadth pair. These relationships are represented by the C and B curves in figure 3-12. The points C_L and B_L reflect limiting points—the maximum cost which managers can bear without going out of business, and the minimum benefit which workers will accept.[44] The distribution of training costs represented by point E corresponds to an equilibrium job/training breadth pair for both sides.

Two examples of the results produced by this model may be presented. In the first case, contrast the C curve above with that for a firm with considerable market power. Such a firm would be able to pass on costs to its customers with the result that the costs borne by managers would be reduced for any share of training costs assumed. Figure 3-13 contrasts two firms with varying power to pass on costs. The monopolistic firm will bear a larger share of the cost; beyond this, jobs and training should be broader.[45]

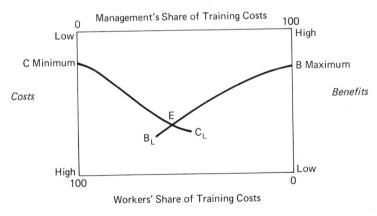

Figure 3–12. The Equilibrium Solution.

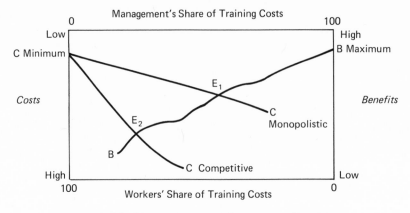

Figure 3-13. Monopolistic and Competitive Equilibria.

In the second case, consider the difference between unorganized and strongly organized labor, particularly in the framework of job-control craft unionism. The assumption of training costs by unorganized and easily substituted workers does not perceptibly affect the individual's employment probabilities. Strongly organized workers, however, would be willing to assume costs in order to safeguard control of the work for themselves. In figure 3-14, this is shown by an upward shift in the benefits curve. Workers' cost share, job and training breadths would all be greater than in an unorganized labor market.

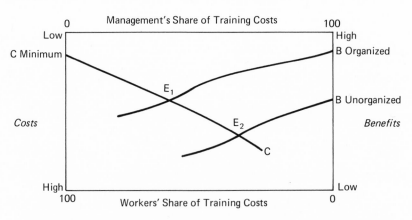

Figure 3-14. Equilibria in Organized and Unorganized Labor Markets.

Conclusion

The model of jobs and training developed in this chapter yields a solution in which job design, total amounts of training, and the apportionment of training costs between workers and employers are determined. Turnover rates, wages, and costs of production—among other variables—would appear in a more complete specification of the model.

The value of the model may best be seen by contrasting it with Becker's dichotomous treatment of the training cost problem. The distinction between internal and external marginal products (which makes little sense anyway until job design is determined) is no longer the cornerstone of the theory. Instead, the preferences of workers and the cost concerns of managements are brought together with the available technology to yield a more comprehensive and realistic picture, less fettered by neoclassical preconceptions about labor markets.

4

Some Case Studies — Applications of the Theory

Case 1: Some Implications for Mobility
of Labor

Let us consider a statistical result which has appeared in the cross-section analysis of labor mobility. Burton and Parker concluded that "the evidence is so compelling in this study that the authors are strongly inclined to view high concentration as a severe impediment to voluntary labor mobility."[1] Although Burton and Parker do not feel that their results are firm enough to form the basis for policies attacking concentrated industries or powerful unions, it is conceivable that injudicious readers might feel otherwise. Such a policy conclusion might constitute a serious error, as it would be based upon a statistical artifact to be expected from our model. Moreover, trust-busting and union-busting might leave the observed quit rates by industry pretty close to their present levels and dispersion.

Concentration of industry is based in part on size economies and barriers to entry imposed by capital costs. These capital costs are related to the capital-intensity of production in various industries. It is pretty clear that there also exists a relationship between the capital-intensity of a productive process and the height of promotion ladders within each enterprise. In brief: K/L affects length of ladders of promotion; K/Q affects concentration; Q/L is relatively high in concentrated industries. To the extent that these three things are interrelated, the Burton-Parker conclusion is challenged.

The influence of the length of job ladders will clearly be felt upon quit rates. Discounted present values of income based upon probable future promotions are likely to be higher within a given ladder (or set of parallel ladders within a production unit) than the income stream resulting from transferring to a new enterprise and starting at the bottom. In brief, most production workers do not take their "place in line" with them when quitting.[2] Of course, exceptions to this general rule would exist—long job ladders are not equally characterized by promotion possibilities. Gaps may exist in the TT line which cannot be or are not (due to economic considerations) filled by the excess training of our model. In these cases, where a discontinuity exists and the subladder at the bottom is short, we would expect higher turnover.

Burton and Parker started with the fifty-nine detailed manufacturing industries of the 1960 census. When account is taken of comparability problems between census and SIC classifications and lack of turnover data for some groups, the number of observations dropped to forty-nine. It is unfortunate that an attempt to test the above hypothesis regarding length of promotion ladders costs us an additional four-sevenths of the sample. Nonetheless, the results suggest support for our hypothesis.

Data on earnings by occupation and industry are available from two sources: the census and industry wage surveys. Census data on earnings are likely to offer an unreliable means for measuring length of job ladders since a variety of turnover impacts will be submerged in them. Thus we chose (at the expense of sample size) to use industry wage survey data.

The measure of promotion possibilities and height of job ladders is based upon the ratio between average straight time hourly earnings for the industry and earnings for entry jobs.[3] This ratio measures the degree to which the "center of gravity" of the industry wage structure lies above its base. For a variety of reasons, including their presence in most industries, janitors' earnings have been selected as the entry figure. It is recognized that the measure is crude—average janitorial earnings should exceed the starting rate—but it conforms to our a priori knowledge of industrial situations, as the comparison below would indicate.

Indices calculated in this fashion are shown below for the twenty-one industries remaining in the Burton-Parker sample.

It is clearly impossible to replicate the Burton-Parker study with only twenty-one observations. Moreover, there is evidence that we do not have a random selection of their industries.[4] Thus we shall present below only the simple correlations between the index of promotion possibilities and the variables in their and our models. Where necessary, each is accompanied by explanatory comments.

Simple Correlations between Index of Length of Promotion Ladders and:[5]

1. Average Hourly Earnings (BLS) + .33 (Average Annual Earnings [census] + .20)

Table 4-1
Examples of Calculating the Ladder Index

	Basic Iron and Steel (Blast furnaces, etc. March 1962)	Motor Vehicles (April 1963)
Average straight-time hourly earnings in the industry	3.17	2.90
Average straight-time hourly earnings of janitors	2.32	2.52
Index of length of promotion ladders	1.37	1.15

Table 4-2
Ladder Indices for 21 Industries

Census Industry	BLS Bulletin Title	Index of Length of Ladders
207	Sawmills (1361, 1455)[a,d]	1.09
216	Glass (1423)	1.17
218	Structural clay products (1459)	1.18
237	Blast furnaces (1358)	1.37
238	Other primary iron and steel (1386-foundries)[d]	1.24
239	Primary non-ferrous (1498-non-ferrous foundries)[d]	1.13
247	Fabricated structural metal (1463-fab steel)	1.31
267	Motor vehicles (1393)	1.15
306	Meat products (1415)[b]	1.16
309	Grain Mill products (1337)	1.02
317	Confectionery (1520)	1.02
329	Tobacco Mfg. (1317 + Report 167)[c]	1.15
347	Textile dyeing & finishing (1527)	1.30
386	Pulp, paper, paperboard mills (1341)	1.17
387	Paper containers (1478)	1.16
406	Synthetic Fibers (Report 143)	1.20
408	Paints and varnishes (1318)	1.09
416	Petroleum refining (Report 143)	1.20
429	Misc. plastic products (1439)	1.10
436	Leather (1378)	1.24
437	Footwear and rubber (1360—all footwear)[d]	1.28

[a]West Coast (1/3 of U.S. Employment) and Southern (1/2 of U.S. total) given weights of 2 and 3 respectively.

[b]Meatpacking (132,000 workers) and meat products (39,000) given these weights.

[c]Cigarettes given weight of 2; Cigars, 1: corresponding to employment ratios shown in *Employment and Earnings.*

[d]For some parts of these industries, rates for "floor boys" or "laborers" in maintenance categories were utilized in absence of "janitor" data.

2. Percentage change in AHE: −.36. Percentage change in AAE: −.50. This supports the idea that, in expanding employment, entry rates are one instrument which firms manipulate rather than rates across the board.
3. Quit rate −.40—as expected
4. New Hire Rate −.47—as expected, since the index reflects (in part) the proportion of jobs which are at entry level.
5. Percentage covered by collective bargaining contracts +.25—a complex phenomenon: workers' desires for job protection and unions' desires to organize stable workforces probably run together.
6. Concentration ratio: +.19—suggested by factors noted above, but quite weak.

7. Average size of firm: +.42

8. Percentage "craftsmen": +.34—as expected

With 20 degrees of freedom, the 5% confidence point is $r \geqslant .423$—thus few of the correlations above are strictly significant. On the other hand, our confidence in the model is increased by the fact that all correlations have the expected sign.

In an independent attempt to evaluate the influence of promotion ladders on labor turnover, data from forty-one industry wage surveys between 1958 and 1965 were pulled together. The ladder index was calculated as before; the only new problem was seasonal adjustment of the quit rates reported, since the surveys refer to different months. A comparison of all manufacturing monthly quits with the seasonally adjusted figures for the 1959-61 period yielded implicit seasonal factors, which were applied to the figures for the various industries. This approach is basically indefensible, but represented the only feasible course.

The seasonally adjusted quit rate was then regressed on the ladder length measure and other variables affecting workers' employment and income expectation and behavior. New hire rates were also introduced on the presumption that jobs are subject to a probationary period from the worker's viewpoint, which is followed by a quit or stay decision. The results appear to be consistent with these hypotheses.

$$Q = \frac{7.61 + .11 \text{ layoff rate} + .97 \text{ new hire rate}}{(3.72) \quad (2.07) \qquad\qquad (5.27)}$$

$$- .43 \text{ total accessions rate} - 2.44 \text{ ladder index}$$
$$(3.10) \qquad\qquad\qquad\qquad (2.31)$$

$$- .10 \text{ average production worker hours per week.}$$
$$(2.93)$$

Values of t are shown in parentheses; R^2 was .7234 significant at the 1% level. Layoff rates and ladder index are significant at the 5% level, the other variables at 1%.

Case 2: The Building Trades

Few industries show as many of the factors in our model so clearly and over so long a period of time as does construction. The market and technological influences and workers' responses to them can in many cases be traced as far back as medieval times. This is particularly the case with work which is characterized by large, discrete projects and an unusual sensitivity to cyclical swings and seasonal factors. It is significant that the extent and strength of trade union organization, especially in the area of training and apprenticeship, are directly related to the severity of these influences.

The historical antecedents of this concern merit a brief discussion. In the Middle Ages, the work of masons, stonecarvers and other crafts was almost entirely centered about large projects—castles, churches, and cathedrals; and many features of the modern trade union movement arose. In particular, the parallels with the nature of organization in the nineteenth-century United States are very strong. Apprenticeship training, the importance of controlling nomadic journeymen, development of ledges or chapters to regulate wages, enforce safety and work rules, maintain the standards of the craft, and protect the workers from abuses of disciplinary regulations—all these were characteristic of medieval industrial relations in construction. The frequency with which projects were halted by war, plague, or depleted treasuries, added to the need for geographical mobility and control of access to the craft. The fact that construction projects requiring craftsmen were large and drew together larger aggregations of craftsmen in one place than did the other, more sedentary guilds, contributed to the strength of these organizations. They were able to wreak havoc with attempts to fix maximum wages in times of labor shortage, much as the building trades treated the guideposts of the 1960s. In all this we see, not a historical curiosity, but workers rationally regulating the scope, training and compensation for their craft.[6]

With the modern proliferation of materials and techniques, new elements have entered the situation on both employers' and workers' sides. On the one hand, technical developments have brought about a series of new techniques: in response there arise a range of rules governing the utilization of new methods. One case in point could be the introduction of spray-painting methods in place of brush work. Rules have been developed covering the problems associated with such a technological threat—upon what kind of work can sprayers be employed, and to what point of efficiency may they be utilized. In this fashion, the older hand techniques are kept competitive with or isolated from the new technology, thereby averting dilution of skill and possible displacement of labor. Strength of organization and political influence over many governmentally financed large projects thus allows the painters to preserve their position in the face of technological change. The characteristics of union organization and the nature of the product market do not require the painters to follow the path of the glass bottle-blowers, who had to cut wages to compete with the machine.

A second feature of the industry should also be explored: the diversity of crafts and the delimitations of their respective jurisdictions. The existence of numerous well-controlled jurisdictions has an internal logic—they can be regarded in the terms of our model as attempts to increase the input coefficients of the various crafts. Imposition of fixed work rules and reduction in the flexibility of intercraft substitution may increase the total man hours worked for the craft, as well as total labor inputs from all crafts. The same logic of preventing substitution, combined with maintenance of average hours of work per man, lies behind restrictions on the number of apprentices to be permitted.[7]

Although such alterations in the input coefficients for various kinds of labor may be in the long run interests of all crafts, there are two reasons why the situation is inherently unstable in the short run. In the first place, it is obviously in the interest of any one group to try to reapportion the total pie—hence the continual jurisdictional poaching which we see.

More fundamentally, however, the possibility of such jurisdictional encroachments and difficulties of demarcation arise from the basic similarity of much of the work performed and the presence of broad training in the respective sectors of the labor force. These conflicts are probably thorniest when elements of the work occur sequentially (as in putting up, plastering, and painting a wall) the points where one craft stops and the other beings may be highly contestable. The existence of excess training above the needs of the current job, coupled with substantial "lateral" transferability implicit in the partitioning of the technology, allows extensive substitutability at the margin. The fact that there exists no necessary distribution of tasks among crafts is revealed by the frequency of agreements wherein a job goes to different crafts in different geographical locations.

There are thus a number of factors impelling the building trades towards broad training of their members—mitigation of the impacts of cyclical and technological changes, restraint of labor supply, elimination of competition from less skilled workers, and the ability to engage in jurisdictional conflicts to maintain or increase the share of the work. All these forces work together to emphasize one primary goal of construction trades unions—the provision of "competent mechanics [who can] command the wages of the jurisdiction."[8]

Before leaving the area of construction crafts, let us avail ourselves of some recent data in an attempt to measure the comparative breadth of work and training for two particular trades. Very little information of the kind required is available, yet many of the points discussed in chapter 3 and above will become clearer through a preliminary effort to quantify some of our ideas.

The Apprenticeship Research Program at Purdue University, in a project supported by the Office of Manpower Research, has recently completed a study of activities performed by several crafts during the period of apprenticeship.[9] A preliminary release showed "activities" and their frequencies in a sample work week for two classes of apprentices: machine tool trades and pipe trades.

These figures are lacking in several respects: one does not know the stage of apprenticeship from which the sample is drawn, and the "frequency" measure refers only to the number of apprentices (out of thirty) performing the activity at least once in the week. Nonetheless, the figures do indicate the broad range of activities performed, as well as the ones that might be said to form the "core" of the job. These are shown in the following figure.

In figure 4-1 one sees that the number of distinct activities performed in the sample week was 104 for pipe trades apprentices, and 64 for those in machine tool trades. The uniformity of the work seems to be less for machine tool trades, inasmuch as the percentages of the group performing given activities are lower throughout. In other words, whereas 26/30 of the pipe people perform the most common activity (cutting pipe), only 19/30 of the machine tool apprentices fall in the equivalent group (drilling).

Various alternative measures of job breadth can be developed from the data underlying the figure:

1. As mentioned above, pipe apprentices show a total of 104 activities versus 64 for machine tools.
2. Weighting the activities by their frequencies, we find that each pipe apprentice did 11.4 different things in this week; each machine tool apprentice, 7.1.
3. If one considers these weighted frequencies as *provisional* indications of the importance of various activities, one can estimate the number of activities which combine to make up various proportions of the total work done. Depending on how one defines the "core" of a job in terms of frequency-weighted activities performed, such distributions would indicate the number of tasks needed to perform the essential activities of the job. Table 4-3 shows the number of discrete activities which comprise various percentages of the total number of activities observed in the survey week for the two trades.

Thus, of the 104 activities observed for pipe trades apprentices, 14 of these filled up half the time as we have provisionally measured it. On the other hand, only 10 different activities make up half of the job of a machine tool apprentice. For the other possible definitions of the core of a job, similar figures are shown. In all three cases, the number of discrete activities forming that percentage of the job is greater for pipe trades than machine tool trades. Thus, *if one had some assurance that these activities were identical-sized elements*, one would be tempted to interpret this as evidence that pipe trades jobs are broader than machine trades jobs. The lower fractions of the group performing each activity in machine tool trades could also be indicative of a higher ratio of total training to the current demands of the job.

One obvious caveat must be stated immediately. It is likely that these activities are not of equal size, and it is not presently possible to measure the differences. For example, by the measure of frequency, used in table 4-3, various equipment maintenance and repair activities may not lie in the *core* of a job—but the ability to perform them may lie at the very heart of the job's demands upon workers.

Table 4-3
Number of Activities Required for Various Percentages of Total Activity

Percentage of Total (activities X Frequencies) Observed	Pipe Trades	Machine Tool Trades
50	14	10
75	37	24
90	70	43

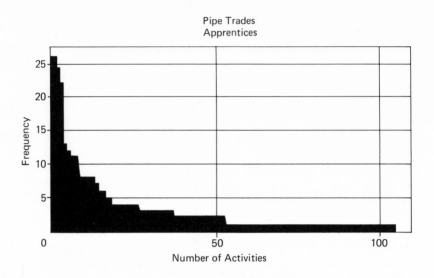

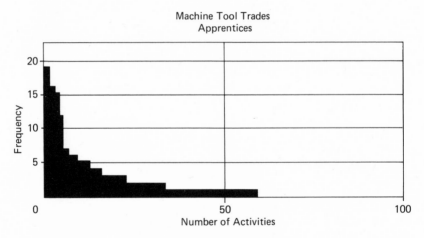

Figure 4-1. Task Frequencies.

Case 3: Medical Care

It is clear that some common parlance "occupations" are simply transitory stages in the dynamic process of training particular segments of the labor force. Thus, although at all times we shall observe the "job" in existence, it is a purely temporary status for the workers involved (apprentices are a case in point). Advancement to the rank and qualifications of journeyman or washing out of the program are the only possible end results.

There are, however, certain sectors of the labor market where such promotion and training relationships do not prevail. Nowhere are well-defined levels of job content and training coupled with the absence of vertical movement so clearly as in the provision of medical services. Medical care in the United States is provided by workers who can easily be ranked according to the complexity and responsibility of their jobs: M.D.'s; registered nurses; medical assistants and technicians of various kinds, and finally, attendants, nurses' aids, and diverse flunkies.[10] In general, and particularly near the top of the ladder, there exists no system of absorption of additional training followed by promotion to the higher-skilled position. Moreover, between M.D.'s and their subordinates occurs a wide gap in the costs of training, a gap parallel to that in complexity of, and responsibility for, the work performed.

It is not technologically necessary that this gulf exist—there are other means of bridging it than those developed in the United States. One such means can be observed in Soviet medicine. The Russians, partly as a historical accident and partly as an adaptation to differing social, economic, and health conditions and commitments have developed a middle stage: the *feldsher*, a semidoctor.[11] In this fashion another job is slotted into the vertical structure. The gap in the hierarchy of skills is thus directly filled, even though upward mobility still does not appear to be of much significance.

For a variety of reasons, this approach has not been followed in the United States. The public, perhaps as a result of conceptions of proper medical care fostered and reinforced by the profession itself, has not been willing to accept "second rate" care. This appears to be the case particularly for those groups which are especially disadvantaged with regard to adequacy of health care. The semidoctor approach might be part of a rational program for ghetto health improvement, but has often encountered community hostility. Much the same could be said for the responsiveness of the "advantaged" population.

In such a situation where (in terms of our model) a technically feasible job option is rejected due to influences in the product market, there remain only two avenues to provision of services. If a set of jobs cannot arise which are more nearly congruent to the tasks and functions to be performed, the forces of the market lead to performance of—more or less—the demanded bundle of services through other forms of job dilution. One means lies in direct dilution of the MD's job—a technique that is costly and technically inefficient, but which forms the basis of the special "doctor-patient relationship" so embedded in American mythology. The second approach lies in obtaining the desired average job-context mix through the use of assistants and other paramedical personnel. Distinct in principle, these two adjustments are hardly opposed to one another in practice, coexisting throughout American medicine.

Direct dilution of the doctor's job is difficult to define in a rigid fashion. As a working definition, we might consider significant job dilution to consist of M.D. performance of tasks which, given appropriate upward referral mechanisms for cases which may require the doctor's special skills and judgment, could be perfectly performed by a lower level worker. As the reader will note, we have entered into a highly emotional area, where physicians and patients alike react adversely to posing the problem in hard economic terms. Many would feel that "to minimize costs, (with particular attention to the use of human capital), subject to: probability times consequences of error—something acceptable" is not even an appropriate formulation of the problem of providing health care. The working definition proposed will, therefore, not be pushed to any extent—it is not, after all, our intent to quantify the extent of job dilution, but merely to suggest that within an economic framework a meaningful definition of such dilution can be developed. The reader is free to decide for himself where inefficient dilution begins.

A number of recent studies have surveyed the content of M.D.'s jobs. It is to be noted that tasks and duties in this area are relatively easily fractionated—jobs can be decomposed straightforwardly into their component subfunctions. The single study to be considered here has the further virtue of containing the physician's own evaluation of the feasibility of one form of job redesign.

Table 4-4 is drawn from a recent study of task delegation among pediatricians (see table source note). The American Academy of Pediatrics surveyed 6,820 pediatricians about both the actual allocation of work between themselves and allied health workers and the importance which they attached to further task delegation.

Judging by the responses of the pediatricians themselves (column 1), there are a number of tasks which clearly can and should be delegated to one sort or another of allied health worker. Dilution of the M.D. job is reflected in the fact that, even for those tasks which pediatricians most strongly felt to be delegable, substantial proportions of the doctors performed them. The doctors' perceptions of a more rational mix of different grades of labor are shown in column 3, when the percentage of practitioners who are or would be delegating the task closely parallels the priorities expressed in column 1.

The results of the pediatric survey suggest that "indirect division of labor" via changes in the skill mix is probably as effective as the classical approach of breaking down jobs. Three-quarters of the respondents felt that greater use of allied health workers would improve either quantity or quality of care: forty percent indicated that both would increase. Thus, even when there exist barriers

Table 4-4
Delegation of Pediatricians' Tasks

Task	Importance and Feasibility of Delegation[a]	Percentage of Practitioners Currently Performing Task	Percentage of Practitioners Who are Delegating or Would Delegate Task
1. Provides Telephone advice-routine questions of child feeding and care	5,772	51	83
2. Provides information re infant bathing, clothing, routines	3,479	69	94
3. Provides telephone advice on handling minor problems of medical care	3,472	44	75
4. Takes and records routine elements of family and social history	2,412	56	80
5. Gives advice on minor problems of feeding, development and behavior	2,341	75	66
6. Provides information re after care of immunizations and vaccinations	1,699	55	23
7. Visits homes for diagnostic observation or evaluation of home	1,467	19	62
8. Takes and records routine elements of past medical history	1,396	66	70
9. Interprets prepared instruction sheet to parents	1,361	52	88
10. Provides advice re management of minor medical problems to office patients	1,259	69	64
11. Takes and records interval medical and developmental history in case of visit for well child care	939	81	66
12. Visits homes for advice or treatment; chronic illness	771	31	55

Table 4-4 (cont.)

Task	Importance and Feasibility of Delegation[a]	Percentage of Practitioners Currently Performing Task	Percentage of Practitioners Who are Delegating or Would Delegate Task
13. Visits schools to obtain & exchange information	761	18	64
14. Obtains venous blood samples	684	49	78
15. Takes & records elements of present illness history	574	76	46
16. Visits mothers of newborn at maternity hospital	509	94	24
17. Performs elements of medical exams for well children beyond body measurements & screening tests	480	90	26
18. Gives advice on adjustment problems to school child	451	92	40
19. Visits homes for advice or treatment: follow-up of acute illness.	447	26	49
20. Visits homes: advice on adjustment & behavior problems	413	12	41
21. Performs some elements of diagnostic examinations of sick children	234	88	23
22. Takes and records interval medical history in case of follow-up visit for illness	187	83	50

[a]Figures are sum of the ranks given for priority of delegation by all pediatricians, i.e. three pts. for a first importance; 2, and 1 for others in a respondents' list.

Source: Dr. Alfred Yankamer, M.D., American Academy of Pediatrics, Subcommittee on Pediatric Manpower.

of various kinds to direct division of labor or the development of new intermediate jobs, it is possible to obtain many of the same results by relative shifts in the input coefficients. Moreover, this method of reducing average job content is associated with the same kinds of costs presented in the model of jobs and training. Two-thirds of the respondents felt that turnover problems and an increased supervisory load posed more or less serious obstacles to expanded utilization of allied health workers. Further, the pediatricians appeared unwilling to assume the costs of training such workers—eighty-four percent of the respondents viewed the unavailability of trained workers as a serious obstacle. The current technically irrational pattern of manpower utilization thus reflects a balance between the benefits (expanded productivity) and the costs (training, supervision, and turnover) of further division of labor and job redesign.

The last case study probably offers the most interesting insights for public policy. Medical manpower "shortages" are well publicized—and the proposed solutions have generally been of the kind which envision training more of the same types of workers now employed. Only recently have more innovative solutions been suggested. Our model of job design underscores the technical flexibility which characterizes this industry—witness the great changes in labor inputs over the last ten or twenty years. Moreover, the reasons why new forms of job design are not adopted when both possible and desirable are best understood in general cost and benefit framework. In the terminology of figure 3-12, C_L lies to the right of B_L in the pediatrics case. Desirable job redesign and introduction of new kinds of jobs might be accomplished through public policies which reduce employers' costs, increase workers' benefits, or directly assume or reimburse the costs of training such workers.

Part 3: Towards an Improved Data Base

5

New Sources of Occupational Information

In this chapter, we shall take up several possible ways by which improved data could be obtained. Beyond the specific techniques, however, lies a single basic question: should employers or individuals be the source of occupational information? We shall consider these in that order.

Employers

A decade ago, the President's Committee to Appraise Employment and Unemployment Statistics came to the following conclusion: "Despite the desirability of increased use of the household survey, the Committee believes that, for detailed information on individual occupations, reliance must be placed on information from employers."[1]

In this connection, the committee recommended that research be commenced on a variety of factors influencing the feasibility and accuracy of employer-based data. Some of that research is discussed below, while parts of this book also constitute research in the area.

In keeping with the Gordon Committee's ideas, which involved exploration of the feasibility of mail sample surveys of employers, the BLS has undertaken a number of pilot industry studies. Thus, in September 1967, they conducted a survey of the communications equipment industry (excluding telephone and telegraph).[2] The survey questionnaire contained thirteen specific clerical titles (with descriptions) and thirty-eight manual occupations, developed to mesh closely with the actual job structure of the industry. Despite such care, it is disturbing that 37.2% of the clerical, and 23.3% of the manual workers reported fell into additional "other" classifications.[a] Beyond these percentages, the author's conversations with corporate officials in the industry revealed dissatisfaction with the clarity and appropriateness of the titles and descriptions on the survey instrument.

A similar study of the computer and accounting machines industry is reported by Gruskin.[3] Despite his caution, he presents a fundamentally optimistic view of employers as a source of data. Whether an average error (as measured by interview follow-up) of 6.3% for only 48 occupational classes justifies such hope is open to question. Although 43% of the occupations were off by less than 5%,

---

[a]The clerical figure rises to 39.2% if "other office machines operations" is not considered a specific title.

28% had errors in excess of 20%. More to the point would be some measure of the errors in occupational groups of differing sizes, but such data are not provided. The most recent study in this series does not even contain estimates of "non-sampling errors."[4] We must remain in the dark.

Goldstein has recently summarized the progress and aspirations of the BLS program to obtain occupational data from firms in manufacturing.[5] Thirty-four different occupational lists with over 1000 titles and definitions are being utilized to obtain detailed industry-specific employment profiles. As Goldstein observes, such data would be extremely valuable for construction of the occupation-industry matrices so vital for planning. The inclusion of a question designed to elicit employer identification of important new occupations might make this an even more valuable forecasting tool. Nevertheless, it must be emphasized that this program will not provide corollary social and economic data on workers, even if it should get us closer to identifying the importance of specific jobs in our economy.

Departing from the line of thought involving sampling enterprises, the Census Bureau has explored the possibilities of utilizing certain current reporting mechanisms to obtain occupational data.[6] This information could perhaps be added to current reports of one sort or another or an additional employer report could be required. Two prominent candidates for selection would be the income tax withholding form (W-2) or the employer's tax form (941). The W-2 approach suffers numerous defects: exclusions in coverage, which amount to 6% or so of employment, multiple W-2's for some workers, and lack of clarity in the date or period to which the response would refer. For these reasons and others, the Census Bureau concludes that the W-2 is not a feasible vehicle for obtaining information. The census document is more favorable to the idea of using the employer reports of F.I.C.A. taxes, which already require a listing of employees by social security number, while the drawbacks listed for W-2's are generally mitigated.

However, useful as such studies of coverage, bench-mark timing, and possible costs are, they do not get at the fundamental problem upon which the value of the data produced will depend—namely, the exact meaning of employers' responses. This difficulty, neglected by the census release, appeared as the major stumbling block in the BLS survey discussed above. This basic obstacle arises from the lack of a satisfactory "language" which would allow employers to meaningfully answer government questionnaires. In this section, we shall focus first upon whether there now exists a well-known set of job titles which could be used. If the answer is no, the next order of business is to explore other routes toward getting occupational data from employers.

Is There a Universally Applicable and Useful
Set of Job Titles and Definitions?

The answer to this question depends in part on what one is looking for in the way of job or occupational information. It is my feeling that current supplies of broad-scope employment information are ample. There are, for example, monthly estimates of employment by the major (and some minor) census social-economic groups. Again, there are frequent reports of production worker employment by industry which tell one a fair amount about the kinds of work involved. In face of the trade-off involved, any new data collection techniques must be aimed at finer detail, less frequently obtained. Possibly one ought to seek the finest conceivable detail—specific jobs—which the BLS or the Census Bureau could aggregate according to their interests. Such raw detail could be stored up so that researchers with interests not met by BLS, BES or census classifications could work upon the numbers themselves to create arrays conforming to their needs.

The number one candidate for recognition as a universally applicable set of job titles would appear to be the *Dictionary of Occupational Titles*. The 1965 edition of the *DOT* does, after all, contain some 21,741 separate defined occupations plus 13,809 synonyms for various occupations. Some observers have even construed it as being exhaustive, and there is language in the *Dictionary* which might support this interpretation.[7]

I suppose that it is part of the conventional wisdom that employers are not overly enthusiastic about the *DOT*. Interviews during 1967 and 1968 with company personnel officers and manpower planners have generally been in support of this view. The author has endeavored to find out why the evaluation of the *DOT* is so adverse. A number of responses are indicative of the problems which corporate personnel have with the *DOT*.[b]

Echoing the response of many others, an airline official stated that the *DOT* was not specific enough to his industry to be of any use. Moreover, he pointed out that job content and distribution of functions among jobs depend upon the size of the city or airport involved. For example, in a small city one adds up a number of clerical, administrative, sales, and public relations functions to make one job, while a large airport would support much finer task subdivision. Pin factories and airports have something in common.

A personnel executive in a tire plant made the point of lack of industry specificity in the *DOT*. He amplified this statement with the observation that the company as a whole had some 100,000 active wage-incentive standards, each of which in some sense defines a "job." These standards take into account product nature, materials, location of the work, and equipment used in defining the amount of product which constitutes a unit of work performed.

The reaction at a company which produces a variety of electronic computation and communication equipment was similar. The *DOT* simply could not reflect the technology—and its pace of change—in this industry, nor did it recognize that there are groups of roughly interchangeable jobs (occupations in the

---

[b]It should be emphasized that the results are in no sense those of a random sample or other survey approach. The contract and Budget Bureau regulations precluded the use of a written questionnaire in this study.

Dictionary terminology) which are combined through worker mobility and movement to create "occupations" within his company. The supreme insult which this manpower planner could level at their own internal information system was that "it is too *DOT*-like."

From a different vantage point, a union research officer observed that the numerous kinds of work performed by industrial electricians (depending on the wide variety of materials and equipment involved) could not be adequately classified by the *DOT*. Curiously enough, the union had found a number of uses for the *DOT* information about the jobs defined. No pretense was made that the information was accurate or relevant to other concerns of the union, but worker characteristics and training estimates have been used in job evaluation disputes and collective bargaining situations.

The net impression from discussions like those above is that the *DOT* is probably not sufficiently flexible or industry specific to be utilized by employers in providing information about jobs.[c] Whether or not this is really the case, one can be certain that employers' current attitudes are not receptive to use of the *DOT* for such purposes. Since informed and understanding cooperation would be crucial to the meaningfulness of any numbers collected, this evaluation of the *DOT* by employers would appear to be a bar against using it in a survey.

A number of similar objections were levied against the job titles and descriptions used in the BLS pilot study of the communications equipment industry discussed above. The relationship of these categories to the *DOT* is unclear, but company officers found the titles did not agree well with the jobs in their plants, were sometimes obsolete, and occasionally even seemed more appropriate to other industries.

What Kinds of Job Information Are Currently Generated by Employers?

It should be obvious that most employers do not act in a vacuum of knowledge about labor markets, be they external or internal to the plant or company. Some of their information (particularly as regards the decision about location of new facilities) is drawn from government and other publications. For the most part, however, companies rely upon data from two sources—internal personnel records and wage surveys of the external markets with which they are concerned. At this juncture, the more interesting of the two is the wage survey.

A wage survey by Company A requires Companies, B,C,D, . . . to organize their internal information (or some part of it) in a fashion meaningful to Company A. In contrast to their evaluations of the *DOT*, most individuals in companies doing wage surveys are sanguine about the clarity of meaning and comparability attained by the job titles for which they requested information.

---

[c]The interesting question of why this is so, since all descriptions are based upon actual plant visits, merits some curiosity.

Naturally, most of the companies conducting individual wage surveys do not seek employment information along with wage and benefit data. As discussed below, this obstacle is not a major one—when such figures are desired, they can be obtained. A few examples will indicate the nature of the company wage survey's geographic and occupational coverage:

1. A company making a variety of electrical and communications products surveys trades and hourly jobs at all its manufacturing, distribution, and headquarters locations. Each survey covers a radius of twenty miles around the particular plant or warehouse.
2. The tire plant reported exchanges of information on certain kinds of production and maintenance jobs with other members of the industry. The extreme specificity of jobs, depending on the precise equipment employed and product worked on, limited the exchanges to information on "basic" jobs.
3. More formal industry-wide wage and employment surveys are known to be made, particularly by trade associations, although the potential detail has not been explored yet. The American Iron and Steel Institute covers almost all of a reasonably well-defined industry, but with very broad job classifications, primarily by contractual labor grades.
4. An interindustry wage survey has as a participant the airline mentioned earlier. This nationwide group of over two dozen companies yields wage and benefit figures—and some employment data—mostly covering clerical workers.

These observations, among others, suggested to the author that there are certain key companies or groups of companies which serve as repositories of wage (and sometimes employment) information from numerous other establishments. Quite possibly, these firms form a network of information which could be exploited, particularly for industry technological trends. This potential data base has a number of drawbacks: the limited range and number of occupations surveyed; the tendency for the surveys to be conducted only by large companies and addressed only to other large companies with which they compete in the labor market; and the general application of surveys only to nonunionized workers.

Nonetheless, there exists a certain group of local employer surveys offering even more hope to the prospector for the mother lode of job data. In these situations, many of the drawbacks have been eliminated,[d] and the strength of employer "information cooperatives" is best revealed.

In a number of major cities, local wage surveys by cooperating employers are carried out on a frequent basis. Exemplary of this class of wage surveys is the following, which the author was privileged to look at fairly closely.

---

[d]For example, companies which do not pull together plant occupational information at the headquarters level (due to the costs of such systems, according to one large firm) do participate in local surveys using their own information.

The group consisted of some four dozen companies and has a history going back to the mid-fifties. Approximately 100 salaried and 80 to 100 hourly job classifications are surveyed every six months, providing information on the whole compensation package. As work-force distributions by wage and benefit levels are given, employment levels can be directly obtained. However, the number of companies is clearly too limited to form a data base even for the particular city, and the criteria for admission to the group exclude small companies and firms which could not "contribute to other firms' knowledge and understanding."

Despite these practical difficulties, such a performance reveals several aspects which could be followed up in more detail. This group of disparate companies has agreed over a long period of time upon a set of titles and definitions which are meaningful to all participants. This was not a simple operation, and it requires continual follow-up and a "living relationship" among the representatives of the various companies. Nonetheless, the results have been so stable and well-defined that the committees involved have developed what amounts to a common job evaluation system for the use of the cooperating group. Tapping this information might be the most important step which statistical agencies and industry advisory committees could take.

Do Such Surveys Offer Immediate Potential As Sources of Occupational Data?

It is however, highly unlikely that local employers' wage surveys could be expanded to cover either a greatly increased geographical area or a much broader range of occupations. The complex of city-wide surveys, industry-wide surveys, and general surveys of the competition by major employers resembles a crazy-quilt as much as anything else. Nonetheless, the following features of these discoveries should be emphasized.

When appropriately motivated, firms can and do organize their personnel information in a fashion which is of use to outsiders. Most frequently, the motivation is in the form of a *quid pro quo* arrangement involving direct or indirect data exchanges. As a corollary, many companies mentioned that they could provide more data for public use if there was thereby an expansion of the data that they can utilize.

Also, when appropriately motivated, employers can and do develop a set of job titles and definitions which are meaningful both to the data supplier and receiver. These categories, moreover, sometimes extend across industry lines.

There would thus seem to exist in the private sector sufficient experience and expertise to overcome the lack of a single, uniformly applicable set of categories. For a certain range of industries, notably those which are highly concentrated, the prospects for employer-generated information are relatively good. In some cases such data are currently being collected; in others, the development process might be encouraged. This approach has the further advantage that the companies can use that classification system which they find most comfortable, while the number of differing standards and definitions which BLS/census would have to decipher is reduced.[e]

A mixed collection survey involving the local group surveys and individual companies' surveys along with trade associations might produce even more information. Smaller companies and plants of nationally important firms not having centralized job information would thus be brought into the net. At this point there is no indication what proportion of employment might be covered by such a system which relied upon the currently existing patterns of information flow. Nor is there a clear indication of the difficulties involved in eliminating overlaps from one group to another. Due to the fact that many of the comparisons would run across industrial boundaries, the occupational detail obtainable would presumably decline.

Inasmuch as the employers' surveys were begun—and presumably would be sustained—primarily due to interest in wage and fringe packages among firms, such a procedure would probably generate excellent information on this aspect of the employment situation. Nonetheless, a great deal of data—age, sex, race, educational attainment—now obtained through CPS/MRLF samples would probably have to be foregone.

Wide areas of the economy would not be covered by such a reprocessing of corporate or trade association surveys. To name but a few—agriculture, self-employed persons, a wide variety of nonindustrial concerns involved with trade and distribution, and the vast majority of persons living in small towns or working in small firms.[f]

There remains a problem—not fully explored by the author—involving certain legal arrangements. The employer wage survey has generally been based upon getting and/or giving data with a promise of confidentiality. On the other hand, it is clear that the purpose for which these numbers are exchanged bears upon the determination of compensation levels of the recipient firm. A plant which is unionized or under threat of unionization would often like to use the data in support of its positions on questions of wages. At this point, the confidential nature of the intercompany relationship will break down, if the company cites the survey in negotiations. If the survey results are actively used to support the company's arguments, it is a refusal to bargain under 8(a)(15) of the NLRA to

[e]In this connection, one should note that employers do some research in this area which yields external benefits. AT&T, for example, developed a series of area occupational wage surveys which were influential when the BLS undertook the same job. Again, one company developed the NEMA job evaluation system, subsequently adopted by the NMTA.

[f]A minor but interesting probable exclusion from cooperative employment surveys—the 110,000 employees of American labor unions!

reject the union's request for data on the survey.[8] The last people that the donor company wants to possess its wage-benefit scales will generally be a labor organization.

What Is the Record for Accuracy in Employer Occupational Information?

If it be conceded that employer-run surveys or employer-generated job titles and definitions cannot be harnessed to our ends, we must face the problem of the comparative accuracy of worker and employer information. Aside from the question of the relative scope and coverage of the two sources, or the extent to which related social, economic, and racial information can be collected, there remains the factual question of accuracy of response on occupational questionnaires.

Concern with the comparative accuracy of worker and employer information goes back at least thirty years. A survey of the Philadelphia labor force in 1938 yielded estimates of the difference between the two responses. When a detailed coding of 233 items was used, disagreement was discovered in 35.5% of the cases. When responses were classified only by nine social-economic groups, the level of disagreement naturally declined but remained at the fairly substantial level of 21.7%.[9]

A similar comparison of employer records with individual's responses was carried out in the wake of the 1960 census.[10] Table 5-1 compares the extent of disagreement found in 1960 with that reported in 1938, classified by major social-economic groups. These groups are only roughly comparable, and differences in their contents are responsible for some of the differences in response error. This would explain some part of the abrupt decline in disagreement for professional workers—which contained in 1938 a group called "semi-professional" which has since been reclassified. For managers, semiskilled workers, and "the servant classes," the extent of difference appears roughly constant. For other groups, there appear to be substantial changes. No significance whatsoever can be attached to the apparent decline in overall disagreement: 22% for seven groups in 1938; 17% for eight groups in 1960. The method of coding the responses was sufficiently different to make the data incomparable. The 1960 figures are based on a "composite" employer report—the primary and secondary job titles and job descriptions—and that one of the four items which best agreed with household response was utilized. Despite this procedure, the level of disagreement remains quite large. Coincidentally, the figure for 1960 is not far from that obtained by comparison of fourteen major industry groups of individual responses and SSA records on the employer: 15.1%.[11]

As seen in table 5-2, the extent of disagreement is increased by abandoning use of the composite employer report.

Table 5-1

Percentage Differences in Response by Social-Economic Group

	1938		1960
Professional	35.1		10.3
Farmers	a		n.a.[b]
Proprietors, Managers and Officials	40.5		35.9
Clerks and Kindred Workers	16.9	(clerical) (sales)	15.3 8.1
Skilled Workers and Foremen	34.3		16.0
Semi-skilled Workers	16.3	(operatives & kindred workers)	13.5
Farm Laborers	a		n.a.[b]
Other Laborers	29.8		46.0
Servant Classes	13.2	(Service Workers)	14.8
Total	21.7		16.8

[a]No farmers in Philadelphia sample.

[b]n.a.–not in ERC.

Sources: Katherine D. Wood, "The Statistical Adequacy of Employer's Occupational Records," *Social Security Bulletin* 2, no. 5 (May 1939): 23. James G. Scoville: *Proceedings of Business and Economic Statistics Section*, American Statistical Association, 1965, p. 319, by permission of the American Statistical Association.

Table 5-2

Percentage Disagreement by Social-Economic Group

	According to:	
	Primary Job Title	Primary Job Description
Professional, technical workers	11.2	12.2
Managers, officials & proprietors	42.6	36.9
Clerical workers	16.6	15.9
Sales workers	10.9	8.2
Craftsmen & foremen	18.2	19.6
Operatives	16.2	16.6
Service workers	15.8	15.6
Laborers except Farm & Mine	50.4	49.0
Total	19.4	18.8

Of course, the above comparisons attest largely to the differences between employer and worker perceptions of the occupation involved and do not go directly to assessment of the accuracy of employer responses. A rough index of such accuracy can be found in the Employer Record Check publication, table A. For eight social-economic groupings, a comparison was made between the employees' primary job title and primary job description. A summary of these results is shown in table 5-3.

The two columns reveal substantial differences by major group in the agreement between titles and descriptions, and some interesting differences depending on the way in which the problem is sliced up. Thus, if the job title was classified as "manager, etc." there was only an 88.8% chance that the associated description would be similarly classified. If, on the other hand, one looks at those descriptions which pertained to managerial jobs, there was near certainty (99.0%) that the associated title was "manager." One should probably assume that the descriptions are more likely to be accurate than the titles, in that they more fully describe the workers' functions. Beyond that, a description of duties, and so on, is presumably more easily classified to the appropriate census group than is a title.

At this stage we should be interested in the disagreement rate which would appear if employers' responses were expected to produce more detailed information than just for eight broad groups. Unfortunately, a direct estimate is not available to substantiate the fear that levels of disagreement—and by implication, levels of accuracy of employer occupational information—would be intolerably high. One can only suggest that two factors seem to be operating behind the title-with-description agreement rates shown in table 5-1: (1) the number of detailed titles—hence the possibility of confusion—in each major census group is inversely correlated with accuracy rate ($r = -.66$); and (2) the number of persons employed (as found in ERC) per title of a major group—an index of how well-known an occupation might be—is directly related to accuracy rate ($r = +.50$).[1,2]

These findings are at best suggestive, in view of the modest number of ob-

Table 5-3
Extent of Agreement Between Titles and Descriptions

	Percentage Agreement:	
Social-Economic Group	Description with Title	Title with Description
Professional, Technical Workers	99.2	96.2
Managers, Officials & Proprietors	88.8	99.0
Clerical Workers	97.6	98.0
Sales Workers	96.6	98.8
Craftsmen & Foremen	94.0	94.4
Operatives	96.5	94.3
Service Workers	99.0	97.8
Laborers Except Farm & Mine	96.2	95.6
Total	96.3	96.3

servations. Nonetheless, they lend support to questions about the accuracy of employer responses about occupations. Any inquiry which sought reasonable amounts of detail would produce a markedly increased level of uncertainty about the value of the data. It is likely that job descriptions would be a more accurate source of data, but sooner or later a general survey of employers would have to rely upon some kind of job titles. In such a case, the resulting data cannot be presumed to be of great accuracy or value.

An Improved Household Survey

In view of the high probability that employers cannot accurately provide the type of detailed information suggested by the model in chapter 3, we must now turn our attention to workers as an alternative source. As suggested by the Wood and Palmer articles, and borne out by the cross-tabulations of the Employer Record Check, there are major differences between workers' perceptions of their occupation—and industry affiliation as well—and those of their employers. There is, however, no inherent reason why this disparity should also characterize workers' descriptions of their *jobs*, as contrasted with their occupations.

For example, one major source of discrepancy between workers' and employers' data arises from the well-known tendency for the former to upgrade themselves on questions of social-economic status. Thus a man may shy from revealing himself as a common laborer, simply due to the pejorative connotations associated with that status. It is not surprising that this pattern prevails, since similar differences arise in checks upon other census information. Thus, low levels of educational attainment and income—primary indicators or determinants of low social-economic status—tend to be most inaccurately reported. Age, perhaps sensitive for other reasons, is also subject to reporting problems: of the estimated 4,850,000 white women in the age groups 50-54 at the 1960 census, 244,000 would appear to have preferred to be the other side of 50 for the census-taker, with only 58,000 reporting ages above their actual.[13]

Despite such well-established inaccuracies in household data, it remains clear that only such data can provide the kinds of related social and economic information vital to analysis within the framework of chapter 3, as well as for other analytical goals. Employers cannot provide some of these data at all, and can provide others only with greatly increased probability of error. In the first class of excluded information would fall, for legal reasons, information on race, and, for obvious reasons, data on income from other employment or from property. In the second general category, an employer survey would likely yield less accurate figures on age, education, or place of residence.

As with employers, let us ask whether there is a current form submitted by individuals which could incorporate occupational data. The most obvious candidate would, of course, be the various income tax forms: no other requirement upon individuals approaches its coverage. Presently only Form 1040 has a space for occupational information; the vast wage earning class with little or no property income which reports on 1040A does not currently submit such information. Thus, in any attempt to evaluate the potential of income tax forms for occupational data, some nineteen million of the seventy-one million returns filed in 1966 escape our purview.

Little use has been made of this information. The first and only time that the occupation reports were published was in 1916 when the personal income tax covered only a few percent of the population. Now, of course, nine-tenths or more of the population are subject to tax. Thus a new look at these data is perhaps desirable. Currently, the data are not policed at all—there are no suggested titles or even a reminder that the blank be filled. In this regard, it is perhaps surprising that the percentage of individuals not reporting occupation is only a bit more than twice that which characterized 1960 census information.

Although taxpayers do report their occupations most of the time, certain differences can be noted between the patterns of these reports and the share of major groups in the labor force.[14] Thus, an unpublished sample analysis of the IRS occupational information, classified by major census groups, can be roughly compared with census family income by occupation of the head of household.[15] If one were to compare broad census groups with incomes high enough to (hopefully) eliminate the 1040A filers—say above $7,000 in the 1960 census—we find that IRS reports might deviate widely for several groups. Professional and clerical occupations seem to be heavily overreported, while managers, craftsmen and operatives receive much less than their actual share of the above $7,000 income group. These comparisons cannot be made exact due to enormous sampling variability, but are suggestive of presence of the social-status biases mentioned earlier.

It is unclear how much of this could be straightened out by adding a list of classifications to the tax form. Problems of reference date for the occupational report, taxpayer determination of primary occupation, and so on, would remain. Nevertheless, future research might profitably explore the use of the income tax returns, particularly as there appears to be some sentiment among enforcement officials that such data would assist them, so that their energies and support might be harnessed. It is thus conceivable that the individual income tax form could ultimately become the vehicle for annual reporting of occupational information.

However, the central purpose of tax forms should not be forgotten. It is most unlikely that anyone would wish to encumber the form with the related social and economic information which we require. Questions about schooling, unionism, and so on are irrelevant; questions on race would be frowned upon and perhaps illegal. Thus for any significant improvement in our knowledge about jobs and employment patterns, we are left with one remaining source—surveys of workers themselves.

Response Accuracy

Naturally, in view of the foregoing discussion, our first concern must be with obtaining accurate information from workers, if they are to be the source. A question on the job performed, associated with a brief description of the tasks and duties performed should yield better data than alternative approaches. One thus avoids an "occupation" question with its built-in bias toward status exaggeration. Moreover, although one might wish to ask for job title, the job description should be a more accurate reflection of the actual facts. Job titles differ among plants and within them: for example, the line between machinists and tool makers titles is highly unclear in practice.[16] It is thus imperative that job titles must be supplemented by corroborating evidence on tasks and duties.

One direct implication of the choice of workers for our information is that much of the survey must be conducted through interviews and not through the mail. This naturally affects the costs of collection, although not as much as it would seem at first sight. For a substantial portion of the labor force, a mailed form should be perfectly acceptable *once the worker has entered the survey*, assuming that something akin to the current CPS panel technique were adopted. Only when a man had changed jobs would another personal interview be needed.

An independent survey. The assumption of the foregoing paragraphs now needs to be made explicit—the survey should be separate from the present CPS. There are good technical reasons for this: the CPS samples and interviews a different universe of the population than the one with which we are concerned—the labor force, particularly the employed. Sampling procedures, timing of interviews, training of interviewers and similar aspects of the proposed survey would differ from those for CPS.

Moreover, the kind and quantity of data would overwhelm or impede the CPS as now constituted. With the exception of special questions tacked on from time to time, the form presently used includes numerous interviewer observations (for example, type and condition of living quarters, race), and about twenty-five direct questions. This leaves considerable room for special surveys to be added—as an example, in December 1968 there were an additional twenty questions for farm workers. Although it would not be impossible to put a dozen job questions in the CPS periodically much as special studies are now appended, this would be at best a poor compromise. To ensure accuracy, the job survey interviewer would want to talk directly to the worker, and not to any household member as does the CPS. There would arise a conflict between the two sets of data in terms of speed and accuracy of collection. It was for similar reasons that separate surveys have been developed to cover the broad areas of housing and health.

New Information. An intensive work-related survey would enable us to obtain the kinds of information required for knowledgeable policy-making on education and training programs and adaptation to technical change. The following suggestions can be made for subjects of inquiry.

1. A description of the job itself should be obtained, which includes the industrial context in which it is imbedded. Furthermore, is this the sole job which the worker holds?
2. Descriptions of the jobs above and below the current job along with the date of promotion to current job would give an index of the quality of promotion possibilities. Moreover, some measure of possibilities for lateral transfer should be obtained. Much of this information is currently available on BES job analysis sheets and might not have to be gathered from the respondents.
3. Wage rate, hours, overtime, and some estimate of fringe benefits would be desirable, as would measures of the stability of employment.
4. The length and nature of the training and education related to the job should be obtained, along with some indication of the excess training which effects the worker's flexibility and mobility.
5. At present we have only meager information on the characteristics of union members: I would urge that respondents be asked about their status in this regard. We should distinguish between "regular members," individuals covered by various union security arrangements who may not be members, and so forth.
6. The customary data on age, race, sex, and formal schooling should be obtained. We might also obtain data on number of dependents, relevant to present and future wars on poverty.[17]

Frequency, Size and Costs. These three items are naturally interconnected and must be considered together. Given a level of costs, the amount of detail obtainable and its sampling variability are clearly related to the sample size. As reliable detailed information is the primary goal, frequency should be sacrificed to a certain point. The size of the sample would not rise proportionately with reductions in frequency, since costs rise as need for interviewers is bunched.

The matter of costs is clearly a relative question. The CPS collects 52,500 interviews monthly at an annual cost of roughly $4.4 million, which works out to roughly $7 per completed schedule.[18] The costs are broken down more specifically in table 5-4. The categories of collection and processing costs can probably be classed as variable costs in their entirety; the remainder presumably contains some fixed costs. Estimates of capacity utilization are lacking, but it is likely that some of the sampling and design costs could be spread further.

A Comparison of Surveys:
Costs and Accuracy

If we take the figure of $7.00 per completed schedule as a constant, invariant with respect to the frequency, lumpiness, or proportion of "reporters" in the

Table 5-4
Cost of Current Population Survey

Category	Total Cost (million dollars)	Costs/Schedule (dollars)
Collection	2.6	4.13
Processing	.5	.79
Survey, Sample Design and Maintenance; Procurement and Overhead	1.3	2.06
	4.4	6.98

Source: Bureau of the Census, Demographic Surveys Division

survey panel, a number of rough estimates can be made of what one is getting for his money. That $7.00 is not a constant is likely, but there is no obvious and easy method for estimating its response to change in the method of surveying. For the purposes of this discussion, we can do no better.

Let us first deal with the question of having "repeaters" in the survey panel. This problem is termed "matching" by statisticians, and is related to two aspects of our current concern. First, the use of matched observations increases the accuracy (or more precisely, reduces the standard error of estimate) of estimates of *period-to-period change* in a series. On the other hand, unmatched surveys yield more accurate estimates of the *levels* of these measures.[19] This brings us to a practical problem—for the purposes to which occupational information is put, is it more desirable to have more confidence in the level of employment in a certain type of work or in the changes of that level? This is not a question which has received notable treatment in the literature. It is my view that academic data users are likely to find accurate levels more desirable; studies of labor force structure, and any studies which rely upon distributions of employment at a point in time appear to fall in this category. Planners—particularly those concerned with the short run—could have a greater interest in confidence about the size and sign of changes.

This latter conclusion, however, is affected by a second factor—the frequency with which the survey is conducted. This factor is itself the sum of two distinguishable effects: (1) the longer the period between survey dates, the higher would be costs of search for the people who form the matching observation;[20] (2) the longer the period between survey dates, the lower will be the correlation coefficients between matched observations at the two dates, upon which the utility of matching is directly dependent.[21] We will pick up this point below.

Let me now turn to accuracy as affected by the size of the survey itself. As should be intuitively obvious, the standard error of estimate declines with the square root of the sample size.[22] We may then calculate quite straightforwardly the standard errors which will characterize occupational/industrial information for various size of samples, pick an arbitrary cutoff point, and then find a benchmark classification to assess the general power of the various survey sizes in comparison with their costs. Table 5-5 does this; the procedures and sources are explained in the notes.

Table 5-5
Characteristics of Current and Hypothetical Surveys

	(1)	(2)	(3)	(4)	(5)	(6)
1. Description of Survey	Occupation by industry sample of 1960 census	An annual survey double the size of present CPS 12-month totals (unmatched)	An annual survey equal in size to CPS (estimates derived from 1960 census)	An annual survey equal in size to CPS (derived from 1968 CPS)	Current annual averages of the monthly CPS	Current monthly CPS Sample
2. Size of Sample	Approximately 3,250,800	1,260,000	630,000	630,000	52,500 per month—averaged	52,500 per month
3. Standard Error of Estimate for:						
a) an estimate of 5,000	280	450	636	n.a.	n.a.	n.a.
b) an estimate of 10,000	390	626	886	1,155	2,000	4,000
c) an estimate of 25,000	620	996	1,408	n.a.	n.a.	n.a.
d) an estimate of 50,000	880	1,413	1,999	2,600	4,000	9,000
e) an estimate of 100,000	(1,200)[a]	1,927	2,725	3,464	5,000[a]	12,000
4. Approximate Size of Estimate for which Its Standard Error Is No More Than Five % of the Estimate	7,000	20,000	34,000	48,000	100,000	750,000
5. Coverage Power of the 5% Criterion:						
a) 1960 Job Content Matrix	100.00	99.93	99.62	99.55	98.76	79.41
b) 1960 census Detailed Occupations	99.88	99.25	97.97	96.61	91.83	20.55[d] 57.34[e]
6. Estimated Cost at $7 Per Schedule	$22.75 mill.	$8.82 mill.	$4.41 mill.	$4.41 mill.	$4.41 mill.	$4.3 mill.[c]

7. Source of Information	1960 Census of Population vol. PC (2) 7C, p. xvi (except for line 3e)	derived from column (1)	derived from column (1)	derived from monthly figures in *Employment and Earnings* as a check on column (3)[b]	*Occupational Employment Statistics*, 1968, table 4	Current Population Survey, 1968

[a]Rough extrapolations or approximations.

[b]Part of differences between columns (4) and (3) is due to Census/CPS differences; part to the fact that N has changed from 1960-68, from .97 to .83 of 1%.

[c]Actual cost.

[d]Excluding n.e.c. and occupations not reported.

[e]Including n.e.c. and occupations not reported.

Several tests are feasible for the desirable level of "coverage power" as shown in line 5 of table 5-5. The figures given there reflect the percentage of total employment which falls, according to two different classifications, into categories meeting the arbitrary (if customary) 5% standard error criterion. As can be seen, the author's proposed job content matrix contains cells of such size that coverage power does not increase markedly with increased sample sizes and costs. However, it should be remembered that the *Job Content* proposals are both tentative and based upon currently available detail—improvements in the data base would certainly be reflected in an increased number of cells.

A more static test is the second shown, where employment in the detailed occupations of the 1960 census is compared with the 5% cutoff point. Much as we might expect, a classification with nearly 300 occupational titles is more sensitive to sample size increases than one with 90 cells, half of which are empty. Switching to an annual survey which would cost roughly the same amount as the current average of monthly data would produce a considerable return in the census format.

Unfortunately, there is no simple, mechanical way to compare the usefulness of various possible survey sizes and frequencies presented in table 5-5. The best that we can do is to watch the 5% cutoff point move in response to changes in the survey's characteristics. Thus, changing to an annual survey would at least halve the size of estimate which fitted the 5% test; doubling the size of the sample would further improve the reliability of small estimates. Moving to an annual survey of one and a quarter million workers, costing nearly nine million dollars, would reduce the size of an estimate with 5% reliability from a level of 100,000 to 20,000. In view of the lower correlations between observations one year apart (and possible increased costs) it is unlikely that matching would lead to substantial further reductions in standard errors.

Is this a large amount to spend? It is clearly not a drop in the bucket of Federal expenditures on data collection, processing, and publication. A more relevant comparison is with current spending on manpower programs that would benefit from improved information on the kinds and characteristics of jobs. 1968 federal appropriations for all manpower-related programs ranging from USES to MDTA amounted to over two billion dollars.[23] Although this comparison does not provide a conclusive case for a new survey, it becomes highly plausible that a thorough study would establish its desirability. Moreover, it is incumbent upon the data users reviewed in chapter 1 to specify the degree of precision which they need. We would then have yardsticks with which to evaluate the possible alternatives presented in table 5-5.

Conclusions and Summary Recommendations

There is a sense in which the theoretical model of chapter 3 marks the major contribution of this report. It became apparent to the author upon venturing forth to study the conceptual bases of various occupational systems that such a survey does not get one very far. Insofar as principles of classification have been clearly developed (by Alba Edwards, J. Gordon, A. Roe), they deal primarily with the way in which existing occupational statistics are to be added together to produce estimates of one or another set of interesting classes. Similarly, our current theories of human capital and occupational choice deal with preexisting specific bundles of work called jobs or occupations. Until now, there has been no model which pulled together technology, management choices, and workers' preferences on the problem of determining what the raw material for all the other analyses will be.

The result of our inquiry is a simplified model which provides a theoretical underpinning for a wide range of recent studies. The picture we see is not the neoclassical bourse-like labor market, but one which embodies bundles or ladders of jobs broadly structured by technology, with jobs of varying sizes and shapes clustered on them. The scope and extent of training associated with each job is an integral part of the model, as is the distribution of the training costs between workers and managements. Factors and influences have been identified and examined which determine the kinds and structuring of the jobs in an enterprise or in an economy. Although the labor market that results is clearly not neoclassical, the model of choice that lies behind it is decidedly so.

Aside from the pleasure that naturally arises from tidying up academic loose ends, what value can be ascribed to the job and training model? In what respects is such a model relevant to problems of occupational classification? In part, the model bears upon the whole question of classification by stressing the interrelationships between job content, wages, turnover, training and the like which are often ignored or forgotten when one starts with a final classification in mind and squeezes the data to fit it. More important, however, is the value of integrating a number of factors (technology, education and training, income, interpersonal status relationships in the workplace) as parts of a single picture, rather than allowing these factors to appear as separable and independent "principles of occupational classification." Data which adequately measure the numerous dimensions of individual jobs are thus seen to be inherently compatible with a wide variety of systems of aggregation. Moreover, such job-based data would be of increased value in research and policy formation, as suggested by the case studies

117

of chapter 4. Naturally, to be useful within the context of the model, such data would have to be of quite fine detail.

This conclusion is not inconsistent with findings of the informal survey of uses and users of occupational data. The pressure among data users was for increased detail and for improved data on the characteristics of work and workers in specific jobs. This statement applies to businessmen, government agencies, and academic users alike. The desire for more detailed and comprehensive data was coupled with hopes for greater frequency of observation than that afforded by the decennial census. Judging from the uses made of occupational data, and the responses of users, it would appear that annual frequency on detailed information would be sufficient for a wide variety of purposes. However, let me suggest that some appropriate organization or forum—perhaps the Federal Statistics Users Conference—should gather more systematic information than that in chapter 1 on the exact nature of the trade-off between detail and frequency.

Under the impressions that an annual survey might suffice, a series of calculations were made in chapter 5 of the payoff (in terms of reductions in standard errors of estimate) to varying amounts of money spent on additional information. In the absence of clear and testable criteria for choice between such alternatives, comparison of the costs with amounts budgeted for federal manpower programs was instructive, if not conclusive. The costs of knowing more about important dimensions of the jobs toward which manpower programs aim are very small in comparison with expenditures on operating programs.

Finally, attention was turned in chapter 5 to the alternative sources of new and improved job and manpower data: employers or workers. Although perhaps unfortunate from an academic point of view, it is likely that this section of the book will receive the most attention, as it differs from the current wisdom (and the current research interests of BLS). Therefore, recognizing matters for what they are, these findings are summarized with greater specificity than for other parts of this study.

1. Employers do not agree that a uniform language about jobs has yet been developed. In particular, they conclude that the DOT could not be the vehicle for the employer occupational data recommended by the Gordon Committee.
2. Current interemployer surveys which seem to have solved the communications problem are not a likely source of data. Problems of coverage, confidentiality, and obtaining related social and economic data seem insurmountable.
3. Moreover, questions can be raised about the accuracy of employer information. The postcensus checks in 1960 are not encouraging in this regard. With only eight broad groups of occupations, one study found a level of disagreement of nearly 4% between job titles and job descriptions (in each case, picking the "most-agreeable" of two titles and two descriptions).
4. Beyond this, there is clearly a need for supplementary data on such things as education, race, age, and so on, which are not likely to come from employers.
5. Hence, we turn our attention to workers as a potential source of new data.

Use of a current form (IRS 1040) is discussed as a means, and rejected for problems of timing, social status bias, and coverage.

6. The only likely source of accurate worker-based data would then seem to be an interview household survey on work performed and other related factors.
7. The number of probable questions in comparison with the number on present CPS indicates that such a survey would need to be independent of CPS. It is likely that information from the two surveys could be meshed through common social and economic questions.
8. Suggested subjects of inquiry are:
   a. Present job description
   b. Cluster of jobs in which present job is located
   c. Wage rate, hours worked, fringes
   d. Length and nature of education and training required or
   e. Relevant to the job
   f. Union status: member, nonmember covered by agreement, and so on
   g. Age, race, sex, formal schooling, number of dependents.

Perspective

In his 1971 presidential address to the American Economic Association, Leontief turned his attention to the current imbalance between high-powered theoretical and statistical models and the small quantities of shopworn data to which they are applied. He predicted that great quantities of new data will be forthcoming in the near future, due largely to pressures from the business sector. Most important, he called upon economists "to take a leading role in shaping this major social enterprise not as someone else's spokesman, but on their own behalf. . . . How can we expect our needs to be satisfied if our voices are not heard?"[1]

This book meets a small part of that call to action. Through examination of the relationships between work, jobs, and workers we have identified a number of salient economic, technical, and educational or training variables which need to be measured for improved manpower and occupational analysis. Although we have presented no final answers, we have focused on the tradeoffs between frequency and detail, between cost and accuracy, which must be faced in designing a system to produce the desired data. If our varied needs as users are to be better met in the future, we must have job-based information, detailed corollary data about the worker, and a system capable of generating these data with appropriate frequency and accuracy.

Notes

Notes to Chapter 1

1. Gary Becker, *Human Capital* (New York: National Bureau of Economic Research) 1964.

2. Jacob Mincer, "On-the-Job Training: Costs, Returns, and Implications," *Journal of Political Economy* 70, no. 5 (October 1962). See below, p. 64 for additional comments.

3. U.S. Department of Labor, Bureau of Employment Security, "Estimates of Worker Traits Characteristics for 4000 Jobs" (Washington, D.C., 1956).

4. R.S. Eckaus, "Economic Criteria for Education and Training," *Review of Economics and Statistics* 46, no. 2 (May 1964).

5. James G. Scoville, "Education and Training Requirements for Occupations," *Review of Economics and Statistics* 48, no. 4 (November 1966).

6. Sidney A. Fine, "The Use of the Dictionary of Occupational Titles as a Source of Estimates of Educational and Training Requirements," *Journal of Human Resources* 3, no. 3 (Summer 1968).

7. Scoville, "Education and Training Requirements," pp. 391-2.

8. See the author's chapter 22, "Manpower Implications" in *Counterbudget*, ed. R. Benson and H. Wolman, (Praeger 1971).

9. Glen Cain, W. Lee Hansen, and Burton A. Weisbrod, "Occupational Classification: As Economic Approach," *Monthly Labor Review* 90, no. 2 (February 1967).

10. Lowell E. Gallaway, "Labor Mobility and Structural Unemployment," *American Economic Review* 53, no. 4 (September 1963).

11. James D. Gwartney, "Discrimination and Income Differentials," *American Economic Review*, 60, no. 3 (June 1970).

12. Derek C. Bok and John T. Dunlop, *Labor and The American Community*, ch. 2 (Simon and Schuster, 1970). For a more exhaustive analysis of these data, see my "Influences on Unionization in the U.S. in 1966," *Industrial Relations* 10, no. 3 (October 1971).

13. Clopper Almon, *The American Economy to 1975*, (New York: Harper & Row, 1966).

14. John Wiley and Sons (1967), pp. 117ff. Throughout this section, documentation is hardly complete. Little attempt is made to sketch the development of ideas and associated literature; much less are subject bibliographies our goal. In general, references are to recent articles, most of which provide reference to earlier writings.

15. A. B. Hollingshead and F. C. Redlich, *Social Class and Mental Illness*, 2nd ed. (New York: John Wiley and Sons, 1964), appendix 2.

16. Alex Inkeles and Peter H. Rossi, "National Comparisons of Occupational Prestige," *American Journal of Sociology*, 61, no. 4 (January 1956): 329-39.

17. J. Michael Armer, "Intersociety and Intrasociety Correlates of Occupational Prestige," *American Journal of Sociology*, 74, no. 1 (July 1968).

18. Ibid., p. 32.

19. See Blau and Duncan, *The American Occupational Structure*, chap. 4. Some exception can be taken to this approach. Norval D. Glenn and Jon P. Alston, "Cultural Distances Among Occupational Categories," *American Sociological Review*, 33, no. 3 (January 1968): 365ff, have shown that the relatively high median income of skilled blue collar workers would fail to predict their basic cultural identity with lower classes.

20. James M. Beshers and Edward O. Laumann, "Social Distance: A Network Approach," *American Sociological Review*, 32, no. 1 (April 1967): 225-36.

21. R. Jay Turner and Morton O. Wagenfeld, "Occupational Mobility and Schizophrenia . . . " *American Sociological Review*, 32, no. 1 (February 1967): 104-13.

22. Eugene S. Uyeki, "Residential Distribution and Stratification, 1950-1960," *American Journal of Sociology* 69, no. 5 (March 1964): 491-98; Edward O. Laumann, "Subjective Social Distance and Urban Occupational Stratification," *American Journal of Sociology* 71, no. 1 (July 1965), pp. 23-36.

23. Robert Hagedorn and Sanford Labovitz, "Participation in Community Associations by Occupation: A Test of Three Theories," *American Sociological Review* 33, no. 2 (April 1968).

24. Robert W. Hodge and Patricia Hodge, "Occupational Assimilation as a Competitive Process," *American Journal of Sociology*, 71, no. 3, (November 1965).

25. Jack Ladinsky, "Occupational Determinants of Geographic Mobility Among Professional Workers," *American Sociological Review* 32, no. 2 (April 1967), pp. 253-64.

26. Amos H. Hawley, "Community Power and Urban Renewal Success," *American Journal of Sociology* 68, no. 4 (January 1963): 422-31.

27. We can get some indication of this effect from a 1965 tabulation of payments to officers (from Office of Labor-Management and Welfare Pension Reports, USDL) per member (1965 Directory of Labor Unions in the U.S.). Representative examples for craft unions are: plumbers ($35.91), carpenters ($17.06); for industrial unions: textile workers ($6.29), shoeworkers ($6.69), UAW ($9.93), rubberworkers ($8.96), steelworkers ($9.93). These numbers are not indicative of total service rendered (as they exclude union employees along with committeemen on the employer's payroll) and are subject to a variety of influences associated with types of union and the nature of its membership. They do, however, provide another argument that such an index as Hawley's is not very valuable in a particular context.

Of course, the census is of no use in this question—union officers are classified as working in the "non-profit membership organization" industry, not as being affiliated with the industry where they "work."

28. Bruce C. Straits, "Community Adoption and Implementation of Urban Renewal," *American Journal of Sociology* 71, no. 1 (July 1965): 77-82.

29. A.H. Hawley, "Reply," *American Journal of Sociology* 71, no. 1 (July 1965).

30. Max Weber, *The Theory of Social and Economic Organization* (New York: Free Press, 1964).

31. Edward Harvey, "Technology and the Structure of Organization," *American Sociological Review* 33, no. 2 (April 1968): 247-59.

32. Omer R. Galle, "Occupational Composition and the Metropolitan Hierarchy: The Inter- and Intra-metropolitan Division of Labor," *American Journal of Sociology* 69, no. 3 (November 1963): 260-69.

33. Ibid., pp. 266-7.

34. Jack P. Gibbs and Harley L. Browning, "The Division of Labor, Technology, and the Organization of Production in Twelve Countries," *American Sociological Review* 31, no. 1 (February 1966): 81-92.

35. Ibid., pp. 88-89.

36. S.M. Lipset, *Political Man* (Garden City, New York: Doubleday and Co., 1960), p. 179.

37. Ibid., p. 198.

38. Ibid., pp. 220-263.

39. Ibid., p. 232ff.

40. Lewis Lipsitz, "Work Life and Political Attitudes: A Study of Manual Workers," *American Political Science Review* 58, no. 4 (December 1964).

41. Leroy N. Reiselbach, "The Demography of the Congressional Vote on Foreign Aid: 1939-1958," *American Political Science Review* 58, no. 3 (September 1964).

42. Nevin R. Frantz, Jr. "The Cluster Concept as a Program in Vocational Education at the Secondary School Level," in *Research in Vocational and Technical Education: Proceedings of a Conference*, eds. Cathleen Quirk & Carol Sheehan (University of Wisconsin: Center for Studies in Vocational & Technical Education, 1967), p. 89.

43. Advisory Council on Education, *Better Options, Better Lives*. Boston, Mass. (November 1968).

44. See, for example, Joseph P. Arnold, "A Study of Recommendations for Technical Education Curricula," in Quirk and Sheehan, eds., *Research in Vocational and Technical Education*, pp. 162-73.

45. "Request for Proposal MA-4" (1968) "Option B Cost Table," p. 27. Subsequent revisions include similar reimbursement procedures.

46. It should be noted that correct assessment of costs *vs.* long run benefits further depends upon information about the promotion possibilities and general future of the job trained for.

47. National Planning Association, Center for Economic Projections, "Informational Requirements for Planning and Projections," Washington, D.C., October 1966 (mimeo), p. 10.

48. Ibid., p. 44. Figures at right do not add to total due to rounding.

Notes to Chapter 2

1. *DOT* 1 (1965): xvii.

2. *DOT* 1 (1965) xviii.

3. For a discussion of the GED and SVP estimates, cf. Sidney A. Fine, "The Use of the Dictionary of Occupational Titles as a Source of Estimates of Educational and Training Requirements." *Journal of Human Resources* 3, no. 3, (Summer 1968), pp. 363-74.

4. *DOT* 1 (1965): xviii.

5. Ibid., footnote.

6. *DOT* 2 (1965): 649-50.

7. Ibid., p. 649.

8. James G. Scoville, "Making Occupational Statistics More Relevant," *Proceedings of the Business and Social Statistics Section* (American Statistical Association, 1965), pp. 321-22.

9. Cf. Sidney A. Fine, "The Nature of Automated Jobs and Their Educational and Training Requirements," (McLean, Va.: Human Sciences Research, Inc., June 1964).

10. Scoville, "Making Occupational Statistics More Relevant," p. 322.

11. *DOT Supplement*, 1966, p. A-5.

12. R.S. Eckaus, "Economic Criteria for Education and Training," *Review of Economics and Statistics* 46, no. 2 (May 1964), and James G. Scoville, "Education and Training Requirements for Occupations," *Review of Economics and Statistics* 48, no. 4, (November, 1966).

13. Sidney A. Fine, "The Use of the Dictionary of Occupational Titles as a Source of Estimates of Educational and Training Requirements," *Journal of Human Resources* 3, no. 3 (Summer 1968).

14. In this regard, a novel use (at least to this author) of the GED and SVP levels can be noted: as supporting evidence for an educational deduction on the Federal Income Tax.

15. U.S. Department of Commerce, *The Classified Index of Occupations and Industries* (Washington, D.C.: U.S. Government Printing Office, 1960).

16. A more exhaustive history is found in J.G. Scoville, "The Development and Relevance of U.S. Occupational Data," *Industrial and Labor Relations Review* 19, no. 1 (October 1965).

17. *Comparative Occupational Statistics for the U.S. 1870-1940*. Emphasis added.

18. Cf: Jerome Gordon, "Occupational Classification: Current Issues and an Interim Solution," *Proceedings of the American Statistical Association*, 1967, Social Statistics Section, pp. 277-88.

R.W. Hodge and P.M. Siegel, "The Classification of Occupations: Some Problems of Sociological Interpretation," *Proceedings of the American Statistical Association*, 1966, Social Statistics Section, pp. 176-208.

J.G. Scoville, "Making Occupational Statistics More Relevant," *Proceedings of the American Statistical Association*, 1965, Business and Economic Statistics Section, pp. 317-22, and "The Development and Relevance of U.S. Occupational Data," *Industrial and Labor Relations Review* 19, no. 1 (October 1965), pp. 70-79.

19. See, for instance: L. Gallaway, "Labor Mobility and Structural Unemployment," *American Economic Review* 53, no. 4 (September 1963). Robert L. Raimon and Vladimir Stoikov, in "The Quality of the Labor Force," *Industrial and Labor Relations Review* 20, no. 3 (April 1967), have also used these groups in attempts to measure the "quality" of the labor force—similar objections can be raised.

20. *International Standard Classification of Occupations* (Geneva: International Labor Office, 1958).

21. Ibid., p. 1.

22. ILO, Working Group on Revision of ISCO, *Working Document: Part 1: Analysis of Proposals* (WG/ISCO 65/2 Part 1) Geneva 1965, p. 5.

23. *ISCO*, p. 3.

24. *ISCO*, p. 6.

25. *ILO, Working Document*, pp. 6-7.

26. Ibid., p. 35.

27. Letter to the author from K.J. Penniment, Assistant Chief Statistician, International Labour Office, November 13, 1967.

28. *Yearbook of Labour Statistics*, p. 3.

29. James G. Scoville, "The Development and Relevance of U.S. Occupational Data," *Industrial and Labor Relations Review* 19, no. 1 (October 1965). I had argued that census groups, although based on socio-economic principles, were lacking from that standpoint and others as well. See J.B. Gordon, "Occupational Classification: Current Issues and an Interim Solution," *Proceedings of the American Statistical Association*, Social Statistics Section (1967).

30. Interesting examples of use of the French "socio-professional" classification are given by M. Brichler, "Classification of the Population by Social and Economic Characteristics—the French Experience and International Recommendations," *Journal of the Royal Statistical Society* (A) 121, pt. II (1958): 161-96: Height and weight of students, mortality, expenditure patterns, and drinking habits all depend on social-economic status.

31. A. Jaffe, "Suggestions for a Supplemental Grouping of the Occupational Classification System," *Estadistica* 15, no. 54 (March 1957): 13-23.

32. U.S. Bureau of the Census, "Methodology and Scores of SES," Working paper 15, 1963.

33. As suggested by Jaffe, in his "Suggestions for a Supplemental Grouping."

34. Gordon, "Occupational Classification," p. 279.

35. Richard Stone, "Multiple Classifications in Social Accounting," *Bulletin of International Statistical Institute* 49, no. 3 (1962): 1-4.

36. Albert J. Reiss et al., *Occupations and Social Status* (New York: Free Press of Glencoe 1961), p. 10.

37. Cf. P. Blau and O.D. Duncan, *The American Occupational Structure*, chapter 4 for an example of this.

38. Anne Roe, *The Psychology of Occupations* (New York: John Wiley & Sons, 1956), p. 145.

39. J.G. Scoville, *The Job Content of the U.S. Economy*, (New York: McGraw-Hill, 1969).

40. Cf. John T. Dunlop, "The Task of Contemporary Wage Theory," in J.T. Dunlop (ed.), *The Theory of Wage Determination* (London: Macmillan, 1957), and E. Robert Livernash, "The Internal Wage Structure," in G.W. Taylor and F.C. Pierson (eds.), *New Concepts in Wage Determination*, (New York: McGraw-Hill, 1957).

41. Note that principles of promotion are notably absent in this case, in contrast with the locomotive example.

42. Glen Cain, W. Leo Hansen, and Burton A. Weisbrod, "Occupational Classification: An Economic Approach," *Monthly Labor Review* 90, no. 2 (February 1967), pp. 49-50.

43. Gladys L. Palmer, "The Convertibility List of Occupations and the Problems of Developing It," *Journal of the American Statistical Association* 34, no. 208 (December 1939): 695. One practical aspect of this difference can be seen in the estimated differences in the size of social economic groups when the two sources are compared. As reported in the 1960 census "Employer Record Check," (table 3) census reports are larger for professionals (9%), sales workers (11%), craftsmen, etc., (3%), and operatives (1%). They are smaller for managers (20%), clerical workers (3%), service workers (5%), and laborers (22%). Roughly speaking, these deviations are directly related to the social status of the occupation.

44. Ibid., p. 697.

45. Ibid., p. 698.

Notes to Chapter 3

1. J.T. Dunlop, "The Task of Contemporary Wage Theory," in J.T. Dunlop, ed., *The Theory of Wage Determination* (London: Macmillan, 1957); E. Robert Livernash , "The Internal Wage Structure," in G.W. Taylor and F.C. Pierson, eds., *New Concepts in Wage Determination* (New York: McGraw-Hill, 1957); Gary Becker, *Human Capital* (New York: National Bureau of Economic Research, 1964); H.M. Gitelman, "An Investment Theory of Wages," *Industrial and Labor Relations Review* 21, no. 3 (April 1968).

2. For a recent survey, see Stephanie White, "The Process of Occupational Choice," *British Journal of Industrial Relations* 6, no. 2 (July 1968), pp. 166-84.

129

3. P.B. Doeringer and M.J. Piore, *Internal Labor Markets and Manpower Analysis*. (Lexington, Massachusetts: D.C. Heath, 1971).

4. *Wealth of Nations*, p. 3, (Modern Library edition).

5. Ibid., pp. 5, 17.

6. J.C.L.S. deSismondi, *Nouveaux Principes d'Economie Politique* 2 (Paris, Delaunay, 1827): 313.

7. Smith, *Wealth of Nations*, pp. 734-5.

8. K.J. Lancaster, "A New Approach to Consumer Theory," *Journal of Political Economy* 74, no. 2 (April 1966), pp. 132-57.

9. Benoit Mandelbrot, "Paretian Distributions and Income Maximization," *Quarterly Journal of Economics* 76, no. 1 (February 1962), pp. 57-85. P. 59: "... we shall assume that each individual must choose *one* of N possible occupations. Naturally, two occupations, that make the same offers to every income-earner, may be considered as being identical."

10. The essence of this school of thought is phrased succinctly: "an individual chooses that occupation for which the present value of his expected income stream is a maximum." Maurice C. Benewitz and Albert Zucker, "Human Capital and Occupational Choice—A Theoretical Model," *Southern Economic Journal* 34, no. 3 (January 1968): 406.

11. Cf. Thorstein Veblen, *The Instinct of Workmanship* (New York: Norton, 1964), pp. 300ff.

12. Max Weber, *The Theory of Social and Economic Organization* (New York: Free Press, 1964), p. 227-8.

13. Veblen, *Instinct of Workmanship*, p. 306.

14. For a more thorough examination of job specialization in brainwork, (especially with regard to coordination), see Chandler Harrison Stevens, Jr., "Information and the Division of Labor," unpublished Ph.D. dissertation, M.I.T., 1967.

15. A.S. Bhalla, "Choosing Techniques: Handpounding vs. Machine-Milling of Rice: An Indian Case," *Oxford Economic Papers*, 17, no. 1 (March 1965), pp. 147-57.

16. A number of the U.N. *Studies in the Economics of Industry* have been utilized in the ILO's *Human Resources for Industrial Development* (Studies and Reports, N.S.#71, Geneva, 1967). One may note, for example, the labor input coefficients given for the fertilizer industry (p. 32). Depending on size of plant, product mix and "feed," man-year requirements per thousand tons of output vary as follows by skill level:

Technical workers	.19 to 1.38
Skilled workers	.90 to 8.35
Unskilled workers	.06 to 6.51

The capital-labor substitutions in cement (p. 36) are of interest also. See also ILO, *Employment Objectives in Economic Development*, appendix III.

17. Cf. Michael J. Piore, "The Impact of the Labor Market upon the Design and Selection of Productive Techniques within the Manufacturing Plant," *Quarterly Journal of Economics* 82, no. 4 (November 1968), pp. 602-20.

18. F.W. Taylor, *Scientific Management* (New York: Harper and Company, 1947). The book first appeared in 1911.

19. National Industrial Conference Board, *The Conference Board Record*, 4, no. 1 (January 1967), pp. 33-42. The survey related to three months' experience by a small group of cooperating employers in Monroe County, New York.

20. A summary discussion of employer adjustments and the costs involved is found in Peter B. Doeringer and Michael J. Piore, "Labor Market Adjustment and Internal Training," *Industrial Relations Research Association*, vol. 18 (1965), pp. 250-63.

21. For a survey of a number of studies indicating the "positive effects on total performance of job and organization designs which lead to responsible autonomous job behavior," see Louis E. Davis, "The Design of Jobs," *Industrial Relations* 6, no. 1 (October 1966): 21-45.

22. See, for example, the study by A.R.N. Marks, cited in R.H. Guest, "Job Enlargement: A Revolution in Job Design," *Personnel Administration* 20 (1957): 12-13.

23. Davis, "Design of Jobs," p. 35, table 2, gives the example of coal mining operators whose absence rate fell roughly 60% under new job design. Another experiment reported two pages later seems to have found the reverse.

24. Encouragement of personal job redesign by workers and a program which broadened promotion possibilities appear to have led to significant reductions in the turnover of the clerical staff of a large manufacturing concern. See Charles L. Hulin, "Effects of Changes in Job-Satisfaction Levels on Employee Turnover," *Journal of Applied Psychology* 52, no. 2 (1968): 122-26.

25. This point, particularly regarding increased training costs, is made by J.F. Biggane and Paul A. Stewart, "Job Enlargement: A Case Study," Bureau of Labor and Management Research Series, no. 25, State University of Iowa, July 1963. Let me note in passing that this study provides an excellent introduction to the case literature of job enlargement.

26. Taylor, *Scientific Management*, p. 82.

27. *Chapters on Machinery and Labor* (Cambridge: Harvard University Press, 1926).

28. Richard Lester, "Pay Differentials by Size of Establishment," *Industrial Relations* 7, no. 1 (October 1967).

29. This range of concerns is treated in more detail (providing numerous references) by Jack Barbash, "Union Interests in Apprenticeship and Other Training Forms," *Journal of Human Resources*, 3, no. 1 (Winter 1968): 63-85.

30. A rough idea of improvement in employment probabilities may be gained by comparison of the overall unemployment rate for "craftsmen, foremen, and kindred workers" for 1956 (3.2%), and that reported by the BAT sample of those who had completed apprenticeship programs (1.6%).

31. Jacob Mincer, "On the Job Training: Costs, Returns, and Implications," *Journal of Political Economy* 70, no. 5 (October 1962), p. 79.

32. See, for example, *National Standards for Carpentry Apprenticeship*, Bureau of Apprenticeship and Training, U.S. Department of Labor, 1965.

33. All estimates are based upon an assumption of full-time work, 40 hours per week.

34. A further exploration and collation of literature is to be found in Victor H. Vroom, *Work and Motivation* (New York: John Wiley, 1964), pp. 126-50. Curiously, none of the three authors noted above receives mention. For a recent study, see Jon M. Shepard, "Functional Specialization and Work Attitudes," *Industrial Relations* 8, no. 2 (February 1969).

35. For examples of the dimensions along which this can be measured, see Eaton H. Conant and Maurice D. Kilbridge, "An Interdisciplinary Analysis of Job Enlargement: Technology, Costs, and Behavioral Implications," *Industrial and Labor Relations Review* 18, no. 3 (April 1965), p. 389.

36. Bureau of Apprenticeship and Training, "Career Patterns of Former Apprentices," Bulletin T-147, March 1959.

37. Ibid., table 8.

38. Garth L. Mangum, *Contributions and Costs of Manpower Development and Training*, Policy Papers in Human Resources and Industrial Relations No. 5 (The Institute of Labor and Industrial Relations of the University of Michigan and Wayne State University), p. 16. Emphasis added.

39. Included are hiring costs for higher job classifications. The optimal "excess training" for a lower-rung job on a ladder depends, in part, upon how the costs of producing a higher-level worker in this fashion compare with the costs of obtaining him in some other fashion.

40. In some circumstances the employer may bear the burden of unrest and agitation which spread in his workforce through having broadly trained—more particularly educated—workers who are more susceptible to such ideologies and movements. This for example arises in the clerical staff of some plants in *very* underdeveloped countries, while the blue-collar work force remains relatively placid.

41. A bit dated but informative introduction to industrial bargaining over job breadth is found in Clifford M. Baumback, "Arbitration of Job Evaluation Disputes," Bureau of Labor and Management Research Series no. 8 (State University of Iowa, April 1957), pp. 10-16.

42. Peter B. Doeringer, "The Structure of Industrial-Type Internal Labor Markets," *Industrial and Labor Relations Review* 20, no. 2, (January 1967), p. 213.

43. Cf. C.R. Walker, "The Problem of the Repetitive Job," *Harvard Business Review* 28, no. 3 (May 1950), pp. 55-6.

44. If the curves should not intersect (C_L to the left of B_L), then the job will not exist unless a third party shares the costs.

45. Note that industry-wide unionization can make the competitive firm's

curve move upward, depending on industry elasticity of demand for the product, thus permitting broader jobs and training.

Notes to Chapter 4

1. John G. Burton, Jr. and John E. Parker, "Interindustry Variations in Voluntary Labor Mobility," *Industrial and Labor Relations Review* 22, no. 2 (January 1969). The author is grateful to Professor Burton for providing the basic data used in their study.

2. There is, of course, nothing new about this observation. It has even made its way into respectable, mainstream economic literature. Cf. Walter Y. Oi, "Labor as a Quasi-Fixed Factor of Production," *Journal of Political Economy* 70, no. 6 (December 1962), pp. 538-55.

3. I am indebted to my colleague, Peter Doeringer, for valuable discussions on this point.

4. They report (p. 213 n) a simple correlation of +.64 between average hourly earnings and percentage unionized; for our subsample of 21, the corresponding figure is +.90.

5. All data except the index are those used by Burton and Parker.

6. For an interesting survey of this topic, see G.G. Coulton, *Medieval Faith and Symbolism* (New York: Harper Torchbooks, 1958), pp. 122-241, passim.

7. A parallel industrial attempt to increase labor inputs via fixing input coefficients is found in the rubber industry, where similar "jurisdictions" have been developed. Thus, a worker in one jurisdiction who may not have a full shift ahead of him cannot usually be shifted into a short-term vacancy in another. Cf. agreement between B.F. Goodrich Co. and local 318, U.R.W., Articles 8 and 27, 1967.

8. Harry C. Bates, *Brick Layers' Century of Craftsmanship*, Bricklayers, Masons, and Plasterers' International Union of America (Washington, D.C., 1955), pp. 2-3.

9. "A Study of the Need for Educational and Training Adjustments in the Apprenticeship Programs for Selected Craft Occupations," USDL Contract No. 81-13-33, directed by Dr. Alfred S. Drew.

10. Cf. Jeffrey H. Weiss, "The Changing Job Structure of Health Manpower," unpublished Ph.D. dissertation, Harvard University, 1966.

11. See Victor W. Sidel, M.D., "Feldshers and 'Feldsherism,' " *New England Journal of Medicine*, 278: 934-40, 981-92 (April 25, May 2) 1968.

Notes to Chapter 5

1. *Report of the President's Committee to Appraise Employment and Unemployment Statistics*, p. 203. (Hereafter called Gordon Committee Report.) Washington, 1962.

2. Robert J. Glenney and Brian McDonald, "Occupations in Radio-TV Communication Equipment Manufacturing," *Monthly Labor Review* 91, no. 6 (June 1968), pp. 63-64.

3. Denis M. Gruskin, "Problems of Gathering Occupational Data by Mail," *Monthly Labor Review* 91, no. 2 (February, 1968), pp. 59-61. Gruskin's optimism is echoed by Myron L. Joseph, "State of the Art in Labor Statistics." *Industrial Relations Research Association Proceedings* 21 (1968): 110.

4. George T. Silvestri, "Experimental survey of occupations in metal working," *Monthly Labor Review* 94, no. 10 (October 1971), pp. 18-20.

5. Harold Goldstein, "The New Federal-State Occupational Employment Statistics Program," *Monthly Labor Review* 94, no. 10 (October 1971), pp. 12-17.

6. Cf. "Job Information from Employers," Census Mimeograph PA-(19), October 6, 1966.

7. "According to the 1949 edition of the *DOT*, Americans are employed in 22,028 different jobs." Victor H. Vroom, *Work and Motivation* (New York: John Wiley, 1964), p. 49. "This Dictionary provides a current inventory of jobs in the American economy . . . " *Dictionary of Occupational Titles* 1 (1965): xiii.

8. See, for example, G.E. and IBEW and Local 2156 (163 NLRB No. 30).

9. Katherine D. Wood, "The Statistical Adequacy of Employers' Occupational Records," *Social Security Bulletin* 2, no. 5 (May 1939): 21-24. Only seven groups were actually used in the latter comparison, as no farmers or farm laborers were found.

10. Bureau of the Census, Series ER 60, no. 6, "The Employer Record Check." For an analysis, see the author's "Making Occupational Statistics More Relevant," *Proceedings of the Business and Economic Statistics Section*, American Statistical Association, December 1965.

11. "Employer Record Check," table 4.

12. Data: Number of detailed titles followed by ERC employment per title (in thousands) for the eight groups: Professionals (68, 64.9), Managers (14, 183.6), Clerical (28, 235.6), Sales (9, 330.6), Craftsmen (61, 100.6), Operatives (53, 174.1), Service Workers (32, 126.3), Laborers (10, 216.1).

13. Census Bureau, "Accuracy of Data on Population Characteristics as measured by Reinterviews," Series ER 60, no. 4 (Washington, 1964), p. 12.

14. These observations are based upon a small sample drawn by the IRS in the early sixties, apparently as a matter of curiosity. Inasmuch as the sample was not statistically random and was very small, the comments in the text are suggestive, not conclusive.

15. *1960 Census of Population*, vol. PC (1) - 1D, table 230.

16. Morris Horowitz and Irwin Herrnstadt, "An Evaluation of the Training of Tool and Die Makers," Report submitted to the Office of Manpower Research, 1969, ch. II, pp. 18-19.

17. Also see J.W. Nixon, "Classification of the Population by Economic Activities," *Journal of the Royal Statistical Society* 124, no. 4, pp. 526-42 for other uses.

18. These figures are low, as they apply to 1968.

19. For further development, see M.H. Hansen, W.N. Hurwitz, and W.G. Madow, *Sample Survey Methods and Theory* (New York: John Wiley, 1965) 2: 274-75.

20. For certain low income or disadvantaged groups, it is clear that these costs would be very great indeed.

21. Hansen, Hurwitz, and Madow, *Sample Survey Methods*, p. 275.

22. Thus, were p_i is the estimated fraction of a group in the labor force, estimated by x_i (number of responses in classification %n (the sample size). Our estimate of the total number of these people in the labor force, X_i equals p_iN, where N is labor force.

Then:
$$\text{var } X_i = \text{var } (p_iN)$$
$$= (\text{var } p)\, N$$
$$= \frac{\text{var } x_iN}{n}$$
$$= \text{var } x_i \cdot \frac{N}{n}$$

23. For details see "The Nation's Manpower Programs" National Manpower Policy Task Force, January, 1969, or the 1969 Budget, appendix K.

Note to Chapter 6

1. Wassily Leontief, "Theoretical Assumptions and Nonobserved Facts," *American Economic Review*, 61, no. 1, (March 1971), p. 7.

Index

About the Author

James G. Scoville received the Ph.D. in economics at Harvard and was an assistant professor there for several years developing much of the material for this book. Since 1969, he has been an associate professor at the Institute of Labor and Industrial Relations at the University of Illinois. Aside from work in the manpower area, he has pursued research on problems of labor in the process of economic development, most recently as a member of the 1971 ILO Employment Strategy mission to Iran. Professor Scoville is the author of *The Job Content of the U.S. Economy, 1940-1970* (1969), editor of *Perspectives on Poverty and Income Distribution* (1971), coeditor with Adolf Sturmthal of *Essays in International Labor* (1972), and author of numerous articles in economics and industrial relations journals.